The Ride of Our Lives

Roadside Lessons of an American Family

The Ride of Our Lives

Roadside Lessons of an American Family

MIKE LEONARD

RANDOM HOUSE
LARGE PRINT

All rights reserved.
Published in the United States of America by Random House Large Print in association with Ballantine Books, New York.
Distributed by Random House, Inc., New York.

All photos courtesy of the author.

Due to space limitations pp. 356–357 constitute an extension of this copyright page.

The Library of Congress has established a Cataloging-in-Publication record for this title.

ISBN-13: 978-0-7393-2590-2
ISBN-10: 0-7393-2590-6

www.randomlargeprint.com

FIRST LARGE PRINT EDITION

10 9 8 7 6 5 4 3 2 1

This Large Print edition published in accord with the standards of the N.A.V.H.

For Cathy—my daydream believer

The Ride of Our Lives

Roadside Lessons of an American Family

One

Walkie-Talkie #1: "Dad . . . where are you?"

Walkie-Talkie #2: "We're one minute away. We got caught at the light. You're at that gas station in the middle of the next block, right?"

Walkie-Talkie #1: "Uhhh, yeah but . . . ummm . . . we have a slight problem . . ."

Walkie-Talkie #2: "What problem?"

Walkie-Talkie #1: "Ummm, Margarita didn't swing wide enough around the gas pump and we ran into a concrete thing. It tore out the bottom of the

RV. What should I do? Margarita's sitting on the ground crying."

Walkie-Talkie #2: "Holy crap."

Less than a half hour into the adventure of a lifetime and the wheels had already come off. Well, maybe not the wheels, but sizable chunks of the rented Winnebago now lay scattered around a convenience-store gas pump in Mesa, Arizona. Big pieces of splintered fiberglass, twisted strips of jagged metal, and in the middle of it all, sitting on the oily pavement, head buried in her hands, was my sobbing daughter-in-law, Margarita.

It was a distressing, stomach-churning sight. It was also moving. Literally. I was in the driver's seat of a second rented RV, a much bigger rig called the Holiday Rambler, and couldn't stop. The entrance to the gas station was too narrow and I was too rattled. Rolling past the accident site, the troubling scene swept by my eyes like a slow panning shot in the movies. The wounded Winnebago was beached on a concrete gas-pump island with three of my family members walking around it in a daze. It was four-thirty in the afternoon on the third day of February, rush hour in snowbird season. The street was clogged with traffic and the drivers were getting pissed, mostly because of us.

"That means the trip is over, right, Jack?"

It was the voice of my mother, eighty-two years

old, with a Ph.D. in pessimism, coming from the back of the Holiday Rambler.

"Jesus, Mary, and Joseph, Marge, nobody died."

That was my eighty-seven-year-old father, the patron saint of hope, launching yet another flimsy balloon of encouragement into a howling hurricane wind.

Jack and Marge, the package of opposites, the plus and minus charges still holding enough juice to light each other up after more than sixty years of married life. They were raised in the same New Jersey neighborhood, share Irish roots, and make each other laugh. Other than that, Jack and Marge are polar extremes. My dad expects the world to work the way it should. He bought into this life believing the sales pitch that all people were made to be good but then he tears open the package, rips away the bubble wrap, and finds another con artist ready to take him to the cleaners. And it still shocks him. Every single time.

My mom, on the other hand, would've been looking out the window and checking her watch wondering why the crook was late. By her calculations the per capita number of creeps and jackasses on the planet is the highest in recorded history, and most of them seem to be in possession of my father's address and phone number. To deal with that distressing situation and to cope with all the other kinds of inevitabilities, including but not limited to horrible diseases, fiery highway collisions, plane crashes, killer bees, and Charles Manson–like home invaders, my mother has developed a philosophy that she calls stinkin' thinkin'. By assuming that all of life's encounters will stink, my mother has managed to stay even keeled when in fact things do end up stinking. When they don't stink she's pleasantly surprised. To better understand how my parents' opposing charges influence their outlook on life, I have prepared this sample conversation.

Jack: "We should have my new boss, Fred, and his wife, Connie, over for dinner."

Marge: "Fred's an asshole."

Jack: "Come on, Marge, you can't say that just because he wears Harvard cufflinks. And why don't you like Connie?"

Marge: "Connie thinks her shit is cake."

Oh yeah, my mom swears. She also likes to down a little booze at the end of the day. My dad hasn't had a drop of liquor in his life. How did they stay together for sixty-plus years? It doesn't compute. Match.com would've built a firewall between their applications. Vegas bookies would've shut down the wedding-anniversary betting line. It's the classic mismatch.

In the right corner, at five foot two, 105 pounds, wearing a white floppy hat, denim jacket, denim shirt, denim pants, and white sneakers over pantyhose . . . with an

undefeated marital fight record of 973–0, all
but three of those victories by knockout . . .
the pride of Paterson, New Jersey . . . The
Cynical Cyclone . . . Marge Leonard.

(crowd roars)

And in the left corner, also from Paterson,
New Jersey, at five foot nine, 160 pounds,
wearing a dark blue jacket trimmed in white

powdered doughnut crumbs and brown coffee stains, winless in sixty years of fighting but still battling . . . The Smiling Slugger . . . Sugar Jack Leonard.

(polite applause)

Another bout between my parents was the last thing I needed as I gripped the steering wheel and scanned the road ahead for a suitable exit route. The rising chorus of car horns was starting to unnerve me. Mesa's rush-hour motorists seemed to be having major problems with the way my RV was taking up both lanes. We were now two blocks past the crash site and in a desperate attempt to find a wide driveway, or an empty lot or a cliff to drive off, I cut my speed again, this time down to ten miles per hour. The car-horn octave level shot into the Roy Orbison range. It's not easy trying to navigate an ocean liner through a rolling city sea of ticked-off people.

I had picked up the gigantic Holiday Rambler only a few hours earlier. It was thirty-seven feet long, twelve feet high, with a huge curved windshield and a large, round, bus driver–type steering wheel. The helpful folks at the dealership had given me an hour-long lesson on how to operate a rig far bigger than the Winnebago, but all that went out the window when the rubber met the road and hostile people started shaking their fists at me. How were they to know that I'm not an RV guy? I'm not even a car guy. I **drive** cars, but I don't **know** cars. Manifold? Carburetor? If it's under the hood, it's over my head.

Last year the front headlight went out on our Volvo wagon. When I drove it up to our small-town service station, two blocks from my Winnetka, Illinois, home, the young mechanic asked me to get back in and pop the hood. I didn't know where the hood popper was. I really didn't. Masking panic with a cocky nod of the head, I found a lever and pulled it back. My seat reclined. The mechanic, with disdain written all over his grease-smeared face, walked over, opened my driver's-side door, reached down near my left leg, and pushed or pulled something. The hood popped. Then he went back to the front of the car and yelled, "Switch on the brights."

Crap.

Looking down at the two levers sprouting from each side of the steering-wheel pipe, I flipped a mental coin and went with the one on the right. Blue water sprayed onto my windshield. The mechanic told me to get out of the car.

That's the kind of idiot who was now at the wheel of the S.S. **Fiasco** as it lurched through a raging urban shitstorm. With the lead vessel already on the rocks, it was now up to me to somehow save the day. Three blocks past where the Winnebago had gone down, I spied a Doubletree Inn with a large driveway leading to what appeared to be a nearly empty back parking lot. To guarantee a sufficiently wide turning radius, I cut our speed to four miles per hour and edged farther into the oncoming traffic lane before swinging the nose of the RV back to the right. This maneuver caused the Roy Orbison car-horn choir to morph into a deafening Phil Spector-esque wall of sound. Concerned about clipping the elevated Doubletree Inn sign with the vehicle's high back end, I glanced over my right shoulder just in time to catch a glimpse of my mother giving somebody the finger.

We cleared the sign, made the turn, and rolled to a stop in a vacant corner of the hotel parking lot, where I turned off the engine and rested my forehead on the huge steering wheel. All was quiet. For five seconds.

"Jack, do you think the man at the gas station can fix it?"

"For crying out loud, Marge, those guys can't fix a Slurpee. You know that."

Of course she knew that. She also knew that my father would take the bait and respond, as he always does, totally unaware that he had been duped once more into becoming an unwitting mule for another load of my mother's stinkin' thinkin'. Now he was the one mouthing those negative words—**nobody at the gas station can help us**—and that's when my resolve started to weaken.

I had always prided myself on staying positive and toughing it out, but these were extreme circumstances and the urge to feel sorry for myself was overpowering. What harm could come from a small dose of self-pity? Lifting my forehead off the steering wheel, I leaned back in the driver's seat, stared out the front window, and softly muttered two simple words: "Why me?" That's all it took. Within seconds I was in a full-blown stinkin' thinkin' funk, convinced that our trip was doomed and that I was a weapon's-grade fool for letting a stupid dream take over my life.

At least I think it was a dream. It happened a few months earlier, in late November, after going to bed feeling sad about my aging parents. They aren't wealthy and had just sold their condo outside San Diego, moving to a less expensive rental home in Phoenix. They were going back to familiar territory, or so they thought, having lived in Scottsdale, Arizona, twenty years earlier. Two decades of explosive growth, however, had rearranged the metropolitan area, changing it from top to bottom. My dad signed a year's lease believing the real-estate agent's pitch that the house was an easy walk to everything. Maybe for Lewis and Clark. It was a disheartening situation made worse upon arrival when my parents discovered that eleven moving boxes had been stolen, as well as most of my mother's jewelry.

My parents didn't deserve that treatment. They're

goofy but good-hearted people, oddly matched yet oddly perfect for each other. They raised four boys in a happy home, lived decent lives, had lots of friends, and always went out of their way to be nice to people who needed a lift. Now the tables were turned and they were the ones in need of a boost. That was evident when they called on the evening of my fifty-sixth birthday. I expected Mom to open the conversation with a mention of my special day. Her first words, instead, were "This place is shit on wheels."

As funny as that sounded, it hurt me to think that my parents, a couple of silly, fun-loving live wires who rose above their humble Paterson, New Jersey, beginnings to make it through a depression, a world war, and more setbacks than they deserved, had now mistakenly steered their creaky old barge into the wrong dock. Too old and too shaken to back it up, they suddenly realized that they were stuck, one stumble away from the nursing home with no one in their neighborhood to talk to and nowhere to go.

Sleep that night was difficult. I live thousands of miles away, have four children of my own, a mortgage, and a busy life as a feature correspondent for the **Today** show on NBC. What could I do to change the facts? My parents were getting very old, and nothing good happens to people who have lived past their expiration date.

The four Leonard children in 1995.

Then, at 3:00 A.M., my eyes snapped open. The solution had come to me in the middle of the night, rumbling in from my subconscious from who knows where. It was a gigantic RV and I was driving it. The dream immediately turned into a plan. I would rent an RV—no, two RVs—round up some of my grown children, drive to Arizona, pick up my parents, and give them one last lap around the country. I would take them to places they'd never seen before: the mountains of New Mexico, the bayous of Louisiana, the ocean cliffs of Rhode Island. I would take them to places they would never see again: their old neighborhood, their college campuses, their parents' graves. Finally, before circling back and driving them into the sunset, I would take my mom and dad to Chicago for the birth of my daughter Megan's baby—my first grandchild, their first great-grandchild.

I got out of bed that morning filled with excitement. Maybe I couldn't solve all of the problems caused by my parents' ill-advised move, but I could do something. I could give them adventure. I could give them mobility. I could give them a month of my time.

The hell I could.

What was I thinking? I'd never driven an RV. Where would I get one? How much would it cost? What if we crashed? What if one of my parents fell or got sick? What if NBC refused to let me take the time off? What if Megan's baby arrived early?

I couldn't do it.

No, I had to do it.

At breakfast that morning my wife, Cathy, tried talking sense into me. She used logic, listing all the potential pitfalls, from the age of my parents to the financial implications for our children if they were to go on the journey. Our oldest son, Matt, and his wife, Margarita, our youngest daughter, Kerry, as well as Megan's husband, Jamie, are all part of the family video production company. Taking them on the road would mean shutting down the business and cutting off their source of income. Brendan, our youngest son, would have to drop out of college for a semester.

But Cathy knew that her logical objections weren't making a dent. We were approaching our thirty-fifth year as a married couple and she had seen that look in my eyes before. Out of the blue, some career-altering idea or lifestyle-changing concept would pop into my head and I'd take the leap. There were lots of failures, some costly, but more often than not things worked out, at times in a big way. It wasn't just an urge to be different, it was . . . and I hate to say this because it's going to sound like New Age self-help crap . . . as if I were being commanded to take those chances.

There was another factor that caused me to take those running leaps of faith. It had to do with the way I came off the assembly line. World War II had just ended and the demand for babies was booming. In our family manufacturing plant, Jack Jr. was the first to roll down the conveyor belt, followed in quick succession by me and then Tim. Labor problems forced a shutdown for five years before issues were re-solved and Kevin was born. Due to limited natural resources, the Leonard boys were manufactured using mostly standard-issue parts. Average height, average build, average looks. Questions have been raised about the materials used to make Kevin, be-cause he was the only Leonard to get good grades in school. For quite a while my mother thought that she might have taken home the wrong baby, but then Kevin started to look more and more like her father, generating a mixture of relief and concern.

With baby factories working triple shifts, orders would occasionally get screwed up. A mislabeled part might fall into the wrong bin and bingo, you've got a

Kevin, Mike, Tim, and Jack in the late 1950s.

pretty girl with mousy hair or a hulking man with a chipmunk voice. Things must have really been out of control during the 1947 shift, because I came off the line programmed with the live-for-today sense of urgency clearly designed for the crate of cicadas awaiting the next insect run. Cicadas, of course, have good reason to buzz through life like there's no tomorrow, struggling through a seventeen-year underground confinement with the knowledge that their fun in the sun would be over after three measly weeks. Then they're dead.

My cicada-like urge to capture the moment was apparent from an early age, as I hurried my brothers to the sledding hill before the snow melted or to the ball field before the skies opened up. It seemed like a curse at first, this clock ticking inside me, but as the years ticked by I gradually realized that the nagging gut-level discomfort causing me to fear the end of the day was also prompting me to make the most of what was left of that day. The curse had become a blessing, and with the clock counting down the days for my mom and dad, that persistent ache to do something about it caused me to make the call and rent the RVs.

Kerry.

In the predawn hours of a January morning, about two months after the RV dream, I kissed my wife good-bye and hustled out to the Winnebago parked in the driveway of my Winnetka, Illinois, home. It was the coldest day of the year, minus twelve degrees, forcing Matt, Margarita, Kerry, and Brendan to move quickly as they loaded in the last of the supplies, great clouds of mist blowing from their mouths. My itch was becoming tempered by apprehension. None of us knew a damn thing about RV travel and yet there we were, poised to shove off into the darkness. For a moment I imagined Columbus must have felt the same type of anxiety as he watched his men hoist the sails. Then I remembered that Columbus didn't have to ask his crew to explain why those big sheets were tied to the tall poles, just as he didn't have to worry about bucking the waves while his father yakked in-cessantly and his mother flipped off the skipper of a passing pirate ship.

Margarita.

Grateful that the engine jumped to life on the subzero morning, I slowly backed the Winnebago out the drive-way, tapped out a few short farewell toots on the horn, and drove away. Our journey had begun. In four days we would be in Arizona, where the other RV and my parents awaited. From Phoenix we would travel to New Mexico, then head east through Texas and Louisiana before moving north, then east again. The schedule was tight, but we figured we could make it as far as New England before turning back and heading to Chicago for the arrival of Megan's baby, due in a month. I was hoping that the joy of welcoming their first great-grandchild into the world, coupled with the memories of the cross-country journey, would lift my parents' spirits long enough to ride out the one-year lease on the Phoenix rental home. After that we would work on getting them relocated.

I looked to my left and saw the silhouette of Chicago's skyline fading into the distance with the sun just peeking over the horizon. The highway traffic was moving slowly in both directions. Sitting next to me, Matt stared out the window. Kerry and Margarita were flipping through magazines at the dinette table. The last I saw of Brendan, all six foot four of him, was less than a minute after we shoved off when he planted one of his size-fifteen running shoes on the back of my seat to boost himself up to the bed above the cab. Picking up my cell phone from a tray-like console near the dashboard, I dialed Megan's number, knowing that she'd already be out of bed. A first-time mother entering the final month of pregnancy is used to seeing the sunrise.

"Hi Dad, what's up?"

"You're up. And that's not normal for the Megan I used to know."

"No kidding," Megan replied. "This baby better be born on time. The no-sleep routine sucks."

"Like you're gonna get sleep after the baby arrives?"

Four-year-old Megan.

"Yeah, I know, but at least I'll have a reason to get up. Now there's nothin' to do. I was just watching some low-rent preacher on one of the cable stations."

"Oh man," I said, "that reminds me of something funny that happened when you were about four. You were playing with a holy card and turned to Cathy and said, 'Mom, do you love God?' And Cathy answered, 'Yes, I love God. Do you love God?' And you went, 'Yeah, I love God but I hate his beard.' "

Megan laughed as I continued reminiscing. "Then right before Kerry was born you went shopping with Cathy and started badgering her about buying baby bottles. Cathy told you that she didn't need bottles because she was going to be nursing. You didn't know what nursing was, and she explained it as best she could while walking down the grocery-store aisle. Cathy said that you were quiet for a minute before blurting out, 'Can you get juice from those things?' "

Megan is a six-foot-tall, blue-eyed genetic combo plate of humor, generosity, impatience, and compassion topped by a great mound of curly brown hair that falls to her shoulders in awesome ringlets. It's a striking hairdo, fashionable yet timeless. Before leaving on the journey I came upon an old photo of a pretty woman in the 1920s, her hair just like Megan's. The woman in the photo was my mother.

"I talked to Moose and Spoose last night," said Megan, referring to my parents by nicknames hung on them years ago by my brother Tim. Mom became "Moose" because at five foot two she's anything but that. Dad got "Spoose" because it rhymed with moose and looked like "spouse." Against all odds the silly names stuck, and now all of my mother's correspondence comes marked by a rubber-stamped image of a large antlered Bullwinkle.

"And I said to Spoose," continued Megan, " 'Next time I see you I'll be in a hospital bed.' He said, 'I've seen you there before.' He was talking about the day I was born. Spoose and Moose got to see me when I was hours old, so it'll be cool when they get to see my child when it's hours old."

"What did my mom say?" I asked.

"Oh, I had some good laughs with her, but she didn't say anything about the baby. It's weird. I thought she'd be really psyched."

"I thought so too," I responded. "Maybe she's just nervous. Are you scared, Meg?"

"No, just excited. The doctor says that everything's the way it should be. The baby seems quiet lately, but I think that happens near the end. I just hope that he or she doesn't decide to come early and you guys miss it."

"Meg, there's no way we'll miss it."

The conversation with Megan made me feel good about riding to my parents' rescue, maybe because I haven't always been the one to do that. I'm not a saint or the perfect son. On countless occasions I've ducked their telephone calls. Why would I want to hear my mom talk about the gall bladder problems of somebody I've never met? How would my life be made better by listening to my dad's six hundredth lecture on all the societal problems caused by people wearing their baseball hats backward? My annoyance stems from a universal truth. As people age, their physical size shrinks while everything else expands in a scary way. Talkers talk more. Complainers complain more. Small idiosyncrasies blossom into bizarre screwball behavior.

Every birthday added a new layer of eccentricity to Mom's already quirky personality. When living in California she once responded to the noise coming from an adjoining property by standing on her balcony and hurling an egg through the neighbor's open window. In her own living room she hung a big, framed photograph of herself and my dad with a group of people that included a man she didn't like. Mom solved the dilemma by taking a big wad of gum out of her mouth and sticking it on the man's face. The gummed-up picture stayed on the wall for years.

While Mom was hiding people's faces with chewing gum, Dad was chasing people into hiding after chewing their ears off. Somehow his conversational "off" button got jammed and since it's such an old model, we can't figure out how to unjam it. Grocery-store baggers, traffic cops, bankers, house painters—it doesn't matter, anybody with a pulse is fair game. He's not picky about the subject matter just as long as it has something to do with the plight of the little man. That's his mission in life, to spread the shocking news that the little man is getting a royal screw job. Through the years we've tried to tell him that this is **not** a major scoop, that the little man has been getting his butt kicked forever. It's the law of the jungle and it's been on the books since Caveman One swindled Caveman Two out of the lucrative Termite Pie distributorship. My dad, however, thinks he can repeal that jungle law simply by swinging through life on his righteous vine yodeling to everyone within earshot for the butt-kicking to stop. It never does. Tarzan Jack keeps swinging, though, swooping down to grab the little man by the waist before turning around just in time to catch the trunk of the tree flush in the face.

And yet there I was, poised to drive a rented RV into the belly of the beast. Every eccentricity, every annoying habit, every repeated story would only be magnified as the miles clicked off and the hours piled up. To be trapped with my parents in a rolling tin can for a whole month would surely come at a cost, especially to my sanity, but this was payback time and I owed a lot. You can't put a price tag on a happy childhood. It's a gift, and for the Leonard boys it came wrapped in a colorful package.

As a little boy I would often walk uptown at the end of the day and wait for all the worn-out commuters to step off the train. My dad was the only man in a suit who was never too tired to race his son home, high-stepping down the small-town sidewalks, weaving through the crowds of businessmen, all the while calling the race like a hyped-up Olympic sportscaster. The course was three blocks

long and we ran it a lot, even on the hottest days of summer. My dad was a good athlete and fast runner and I was only seven or eight, but somehow I always managed to eke out a win, always in a dramatic, come-from-behind photo finish.

When Dad went on an occasional business trip, Mom would sometimes take us for an after-dinner spin around the neighborhood. The family vehicle must have been purchased from a fleet of used cop cars, because it had a powerful searchlight that could be rotated and controlled by a dashboard-mounted handle. After dinner Jack, Timmy, and I would be quietly going about our normal business, perhaps trying for the umpteenth time to fit marbles into Kevin's nostrils, when my mom would walk in and say, "Hey boys, wanna take a ride through the

Businessman Jack.

neighborhood? Maybe we can beam the searchlight into the Nevards' house and see Hugo in his underwear again." And sometimes we would see him half naked, touching off an explosion of high-pitched giggling from the backseat of an old sedan as it cruised down a quiet, tree-lined suburban street, a young, redhaired woman at the wheel, pounding the dashboard in hysterical laughter.

Half a century later I'm the one at the wheel heading for a rendezvous with two old people waiting to embark on their last great adventure. There was little conversation as the Winnebago descended from the mountains that surround Phoenix and the neighboring communities. It was my turn with the CD player, and John Prine's lyrics filled the silence:

**"The scientific nature of the ordinary man
Is to go on out and do the best you can."**

The song is relatively new, but hearing Prine's voice brought me back to our Arizona days. Cathy and I moved to Phoenix after getting married, and three of our four children were born there. We stayed ten years, spending most of that time struggling to make ends meet while raising our kids and listening to John Prine sing about people just like us. I was the common man doing common jobs: construction, sales, retail, and the list goes on. Before Prine found his niche as a songwriter he was a mailman. We knew that he knew exactly how we felt. My niche would eventually be found, but not until the age of thirty, when I landed my first TV job. A year and a half later, NBC came calling and off we went.

Another thought came to mind as I drove the Winnebago down the winding mountain road. It was the memory of our second child, the first girl in the Leonard family. She had curly brown hair and bright blue eyes. Even as a toddler her sweet, independent manner, coupled with a sense of humor, gave her a special glow. When she was about two years old we went to a friend's house for a barbecue. The family had a pool. After dinner some of the men started playing a game of water basketball in the shallow end. I joined them. Cathy stayed inside with the other wives and a huge crowd of children. It was dark. One of the men threw the basketball to me, but the pass sailed over my head and into the deep end. Dipping below the surface, I pushed off the side and propelled my body toward where the ball had landed, staying underwater the whole time. There was something ahead of me, obscuring one of the underwater lights. As I glided closer, the object came into focus—first the dress, waving in the currents, then the little red sandals, and finally the face. It was my daughter. Grabbing her by the waist, I quickly lifted her body above the surface. Water gushed from her mouth. A moment later she started crying. Nobody had seen her leave the house or fall into the pool seconds before the ball flew over my head. What if that pass had been good? What if I'd caught it? Those were my thoughts as I stood trembling in the darkness, my arms wrapped tightly around my little girl.

Another generation had passed, and now two RVs inched down a narrow Phoenix street toward an old couple standing by a row of suitcases. The clock was ticking. There was no time to waste. If all went as planned, they'd be in Chicago when the little girl who fell into the pool, my daughter Megan, gave birth to their first great-grandchild.

This was to be my gift to them.

Their final hurrah.

Their last lap.

The ride of their lives.

Thirty minutes later, the Winnebago was in pieces.

Two

I left my parents in the Holiday Rambler and walked back to the crash site. By the time I got there, Matt had moved the Winnebago from its wedged position between the rows of gas pumps to an empty area off to the side of the convenience mart. The RV seemed drivable, but most of the fiberglass storage bins had been ripped from its lower left side. Strips of metal hung this way and that. Kerry and Brendan had cleaned up most of the broken pieces and transferred the luggage and supplies to the inside of the RV. Margarita was walking around in little circles, still shaky from driving into the concrete barrier. After trying to console her by saying that the accident could have happened to any of us, I climbed into the Winnebago to assess our options.

Kerry, my twenty-five-year-old daughter and the trip's designated navigator, had succeeded in making contact with Winnebago's main office and she handed the cell phone to me. The woman on the line had already described the damage to a mechanic at a nearby RV repair shop, who said that the torn-out storage section could be covered with temporary siding. If we got the vehicle to him first thing in the morning we could be back on the road by noon. Nothing was said about the cost, which I guessed to be in the thousands. At that moment it didn't matter. The trip had been saved.

It was close to 6:00 P.M., and the decision was made to drive the RVs to the repair shop that evening and look for a nearby spot to set up camp. There was still some cleanup work to do, so I walked back to the Holiday Rambler to check on my parents. I had left them an hour ago, more than enough time for all hell to break loose, especially if Mom had discovered where the wine was stored. Just to get the record straight, my mom isn't a problem drinker. Let me rephrase that. My mom's drinking isn't a problem . . . unless you happen to be my dad. Even under normal circumstances her feisty, wise-ass nature pushes Dad's stress needle to the upper regions of the tolerance scale. Add wine, beer, or vodka to the equation and the numbers go through the roof. It's tricky math, but after many years of observation my brothers and I came up with this formula:

One belt equals my mother squared.
Two belts equals my mother cubed.
Three belts equals Smokin' Joe Frazier in my
mother's body.

Dad, a teetotaler his entire life, has no chance in these alcohol-fueled situations. His only defense is to sandbag his sanity and ride out the pounding.

After walking back to the Holiday Rambler, I was relieved to see that my mother hadn't yet unearthed the cache of wine. Just finding the cabinet where it was stored would have been difficult with all of their belongings piled inside the RV. I had pleaded with my parents to pack light, but after pulling up to their rental home earlier in the day and seeing the mountain of suitcases, duffel bags, cardboard boxes, and paper sacks, one of them holding a nearly empty carton of milk, I found myself wishing for a Dial-A-Sherpa service to help with the load.

How many dress shoes does an elderly retiree need for RV travel? At least six pairs, I discovered. A bunch of sports coats too. And ties. Piles of ties. Hey, you've got to be ready. An important business meeting might pop up in the parking lot of some rural Piggly Wiggly, which is probably why my dad also brought along two huge briefcases stuffed with ancient, yellowed documents from deals closed three decades earlier.

"Hey Mike, see the pants I bought? Three pairs for twenty-seven dollars."

Dad had opened a suitcase and was proudly holding a folded stack of light blue material. Mom stood behind him with a pained look on her face.

"Jack, those are sheets!"

"I knew that, Marge," Dad replied, "I just grabbed the wrong pile. Here they are. What do you think, Mike?"

Mom's pained expression grew worse.

"For God's sakes Jack, those are sheets too!"

Dad looked at me with a sheepish grin.

"Hey Mike," he whispered, "don't grow old."

Just then a horn tooted and the Winnebago pulled up next to us. My kids had removed most of the hanging strips of metal and bent the others upward so they wouldn't scrape the road. Matt was driving, and he motioned for me to follow him out of the parking lot. Rush hour was over and the traffic was light, so we took our time making wide right-hand turns onto the main drag. No fist shaking. No horn honking. Fifteen minutes later the repair shop came into view and we started searching for a place to park the RVs for the night.

It didn't take long. Like an apparition, a campsite appeared as if it were some kind of sign from above. Actually it **was** a sign from above, a really big one towering over a row of palm trees right down the street from the repair shop. The sign said "Camping World." Over the centuries the camping gene had been bred out of the Leonard family, so none of us knew that Camping World was a national chain of stores catering to the kind of people who never have to draw straws to see who will broom the small spider off the kitchen ceiling. Our coat of arms—if we had one—would show a cowering stick figure aiming a can of Raid at a tiny smudge with legs. The idea of stepping barefoot into a body of water without a concrete and/or sandy bottom is too frightening to consider. Childhood memories persist of a forced summer-camp swim in a muddy-bottomed Wisconsin lake. To avoid harassment and perhaps a "de-pantsment" from the older campers, I pretended to be having the time of my life, smiling chest deep in the leech-infested waters while bicycling my legs at supersonic speed. Huck Finn would have beat my ass with a canoe paddle.

I have a deal with nature. You stay out of my way and I'll stay out of yours. I've held up my side of the bargain. The animals haven't. Somehow a bird got into our suburban basement a few years back. It freaked out the whole family. Nobody would go down there—a problem, because that's where we kept the washer and dryer and we were soon out of clean clothes. This bird was holding us hostage, and being the patriarch of the clan, and drawing the short straw, I was sent down to negotiate—birdseed and a safe passage out for clean underpants, no questions

asked. Not knowing what kind of bargaining mood
the bird was in, I played it cautiously, wearing a large
overcoat, a hockey helmet with full face mask, and
big, padded hockey gloves. In each gloved hand I carried a tennis racquet. The bird wasn't talking. It was
dive-bombing. I raced back up the stairs and called
for reinforcements. A local cop came and opened a
basement window. The bird flew away. It must have
seen the cop's holster.

On another occasion, squirrels chewed through
part of our roof and took up residence in the attic.
Apparently they were thinking long-term lease because when my wife went up to check, she found
acorns in a partially opened dresser drawer. That
pissed me off. Squirrels have trees. We have houses.
I don't wedge my weekly supply of American cheese
slices into one of their lousy knotholes. The attic in-
vasion prompted another call to the exterminator.
We have become friendly. A big guy with a goatee,
his name is Kevin. Lately he's taken to wearing
Western outfits and sometimes a cowboy hat. Kevin
said that we had to replace the roof with thicker,
nonchewable material. He also recommended rein-
sulating the attic, because the squirrels had urinated
on the old insulation and now the scent was attract-
ing more squirrels.

That's screwed up, I told Kevin. I don't hang
around men's urinals, although I did meet Bob Costas,
the American broadcasting icon, in a men's room in
Seoul, Korea. That encounter led to a job doing fea-

ture stories for Bob's Olympic program and later for his NFL pregame show. Bob's a good guy, talented, funny, and fond of Wiffle Ball, the scaled-down baseball game played with a plastic ball full of holes. On two separate occasions Bob and his kids have flown to Chicago to play in my elaborate front-yard Wiffle Ball Stadium, complete with home-run fences, foul poles, even an electronic scoreboard. Costas is big-time famous, but mixes easily with regular folk. That was apparent from our first meeting in the men's room and that's why I was drawn to him. The scent of urine had nothing to do with it. At least for me it didn't; I can't speak for Bob.

Our front yard Wiffle Ball stadium. Some assembly required.

The sun was setting by the time we maneuvered the vehicles into a far-off region of the Camping World parking lot. That's when I heard it—a kind of pulsating, whining noise mixed with a steady rhythmic clacking. When I opened the door, the racket got much louder. Our parking-lot campsite was in the shadows of a highway overpass, kitty-corner to a railroad crossing. A freight train was rumbling by, blasting its horn repeatedly. The train seemed to have at least seven thousand cars. I stepped back inside and closed the door.

"Where's the vino?"

"Oh, Jesus."

The elders had spoken. The familiar call and response had rung out. Nightly services at the Leonard Church of the Absurd had begun with the discovery of a wine bottle.

"Where's the corkscrew?" Mom asked.

"I don't know." Dad nervously scratched his head. "I might have accidentally thrown it out with that carton of milk Mike told me to ditch."

"You've got to be kidding," Mom moaned. "Well, you're just gonna have to open it with your teeth then."

Elder Jack started scratching his head with even greater vigor. Elder Marge began rummaging through her huge purse for a corkscrew. They sat across from each other at the dinette table in the kitchen area of the Holiday Rambler, a class-A recreational vehicle with a hydraulic system that pushes the sides outward, doubling the interior living space when parked. The big master bedroom in the rear has a queen-size bed, a large closet with a mirrored sliding door, and a TV console full of drawers and storage compartments. A sink, shower stall, and small bathroom take up a middle section that is walled off from the main area, which includes a full kitchen, a dinette table, a big couch that converts into a bed, and two swiveling easy chairs. Above the curved front windshield, curtained for privacy, a flat-panel TV connects to a DVD player.

As my mother continued searching for a corkscrew, the RV door opened. Kerry climbed aboard carrying two big grocery bags filled with supplies for our first dinner on the road. Five years younger and three inches shorter than her sister Megan, she made her mark in the family by being a fountain of enthusiasm, brightening the scene with her curly blond hair, blue eyes, pretty face, and big laugh.

"Wow, look at the size of this place," Kerry exclaimed, "you guys are living it up!"

"Yeah," Mom shot back with a chuckle. "I feel like Puff Daddy."

Kerry's laugh filled the RV. There's something really funny about an eighty-two-year-old woman dropping references to hip-hop impresarios, fashion designers, rock stars, and other pop-culture figures.

My mother does it all the time. Nothing sneaks by her.

"Puff Baby? Who the hell is Puff Baby?"

"It's Puff Daddy, Jack, Puff Daddy," lectured my mom. "He's the guy who went out with J-Lo."

"Why the hell would anybody care about somebody named Puffy Man or Jell-O?" my dad argued.

Brendan.

"This world has gone nuts."

"It's 'J-Lo,'" laughed Kerry, "and Puff Daddy is now P. Diddy, but probably not for long. By the way, Moose, I have a corkscrew in case you were looking for one."

"Oh, great!"

"Oh, Jesus."

The second call and response from the church elders came just as Matt, Margarita, and Brendan entered the Holiday Rambler, each carrying a bag of supplies.

"Man, this is unbelievable!" Brendan gushed. "Who sleeps where?"

"Your grandparents have the back bedroom," I replied, "I'm bunking out here. This couch turns into a bed. It's nice, eh?"

Kerry pulled the cork on a bottle of inexpensive red wine. My mother gave her a nod of approval, then called out to my nineteen-year-old son.

"Hey Brendan, look at us, we're movie stars. I'm Puff Daddy and he's Michael Jackson."

With that my mother quickly turned to my dad and gave him an elaborate Michael Jackson–style peace sign. Everybody roared with laughter.

"It's P. Diddy," I corrected. "And I was just reading about Michael Jackson the other day. Apparently he's a big fan of the Three Stooges, so he can't be too bad."

"Those guys can really belt out a tune," my father interjected, "but I like the Irish Tenors better."

Then he started singing.

**"Oh Danny Boy, the pipes the pipes are
calling
From glen to glen and down the mountain-
side . . ."**

"Jack," my mom shouted, "Mike said 'Three Stooges,' not 'Three Tenors.' When we get back from this trip you're going to the doctor and getting a wad of gum."

Margarita, Matt's wife of three years, shot me a look of bemused confusion.

"My mother thinks hearing aids look like wads of gum stuck in people's ears," I explained. "My dad has been having trouble lately with his ears."

"Mostly, this one," said my father, pointing to the right side of his head. "Marge has been working on her left hook and she's been rocking me pretty good lately."

"Maybe you've got something stuck in there," Mom fired back. "Remember that champagne cork we couldn't find a few months ago? I think it flew into your ear."

Dad gave a look of phony exasperation. "Marge, I've been dodgin' corks my whole life. Especially these last few months. I feel like I'm in a meteor shower sometimes."

"That reminds me of another Megan story," I interrupted as my parents made funny faces at each other. "She was about four and picked up the phone when it was ringing. Some guy wanted to talk to me and Meg kept asking who was calling. For whatever reason the guy wouldn't give his name, and finally Meg got pissed and said, 'What's wrong? Do you have a banana in your ear?'"

More laughter rolled through the RV.

"Megan was a wiseass even then!" exclaimed Brendan.

"Jeez, I wonder where she got it," said my father as he rolled his eyes and tipped his head in Mom's direction.

The talking and the laughing continued through our simple dinner of pasta on paper plates washed down with wine for the women, beer for Matt, Sprite for Brendan, vodka for me, and water for my dad.

"Hey, anybody want the rest of this Hershey Bar? I just wanted a little bit for dessert."

Mom lifted her half-eaten candy bar up in the air.

"Don't take it!" Dad shouted. "I learned a long time ago not to accept any chocolate from Marge."

"Oh, she was a jerk," muttered my mother as she folded the wrapper around what was left of the Hershey Bar and stuck it in her purse. "She deserved it."

"Who deserved what?" asked Matt.

"Oh, this crummy teacher, Miss Sullivan," continued my mom, "back when I was in college at Saint Elizabeth's in New Jersey. I was a home economics major, and . . ."

"What's home economics?" Brendan asked.

"That's what I've been asking for sixty years!" bellowed my father. "It's supposed to mean you know something about cooking and sewing, but I've seen nothin' but canned food and buttonless shirts."

"It wasn't my bag," Mom said flatly. "Anyway, we had to live in a practice house on the campus for about six weeks. Franny Gallagher was my roommate and the weirdo teacher, Miss Sullivan, had her own room. Each week we had different jobs—cook, assistant cook, dessert cook, waitress, whatever— and we had to live on a budget. It was the last week and I got ticked off one night and told Franny that I was fed up with Sullivan. We were dessert cooks that week and I said, 'Why don't we get some Ex-Lax and frost her piece with it?' Franny agreed,

Marge at college.

so we sent a stooge on the bus to Morristown to get
some Ex-Lax, Maggie Gallotti; she was nice. She
was real nice."

I had heard the story before but never grew tired
of listening to my eighty-two-year-old mother juice
up her sentences with terms like "it wasn't my bag" or
"weirdo" or "stooge." I looked out the window. It was
dark. A freight train was clacking by. The same train?
Mom continued with her description of the cake
caper.

"We melted sixteen squares of Ex-Lax and mixed it

with confectionary sugar so it would match the other frosting. Sixteen squares! Normally when we baked a cake we would bring it out at the end of the meal whole and the teacher would cut it up and pass the pieces around. This time we couldn't do that, so we cut up the cake, frosted one of the pieces with the Ex-Lax, and then put them all on little plates. Well, she walked into the kitchen and blew her top yelling, 'You're not supposed to slice the cake!' Then she started moving the pieces around and we freaked out, all of our eyes following that one piece. Finally she leaves and goes back to the table and we bring the plates out and give her the piece. And then she had about three cups of coffee with the cake and I'm thinking she's gonna have an explosion. She went to bed and it started. The toilet flushed all night long. At one point, in the middle of the night, Franny whispered, 'Margie, what if she dies?' And I said, 'Oh, I didn't think about that.' And I got kind of scared."

Mom laughed at the thought. Everybody else laughed at the thought of this little woman in her eighties laughing at the thought of possibly killing her home economics teacher with Ex-Lax.

"So the next morning at breakfast she looks like hell and says, 'Was anyone ill last night? I feel terrible.' I mumbled something like, 'Well I didn't feel so good either. I think it was the fish.' Sullivan never caught on. She had a meeting at Columbia in New York that day and took off on the train. We had a train station right on the edge of our campus, not far from the house we were living in. I knew she was supposed to come back later in the day, so a few of us watched from my window in the house. At about four o'clock the train arrived and she got off and tore through the field to get to the toilet. I don't know if she made it in time."

The memory of that scene caused Mom to double up with laughter and Dad to spring from his chair. Her mention of a toilet had triggered his internal jukebox to drop the needle on another dusty record from his vintage collection of bizarre songs for any and all occasions. He began to sing:

"Passengers will please refrain from flushing toilets while the train
Is standing in the station, I love you."

This jacked the volume of laughter even higher.

"What's with those lyrics?" cried Matt. "How does going to the bathroom connect with romance? That 'I love you' part is the biggest plot twist since **Usual Suspects**."

"What did they sing?" Dad asked as he returned to his seat at the dinette table.

"No, it's a movie," Matt explained. "It came out about ten years ago and had this big surprise near the end when . . . well, it was just . . . you know, kind of out of the blue and . . . never mind . . . I just wasn't expecting the lyrics to go from flushing toilets to 'I love you.' "

Dad smiled and leaned back in his chair. "What a treat for us," he said. "We had a little bump in the road today, but everything will go smooth tomorrow. What's the schedule?"

"Well, the kids will take the Winnebago to the repair shop first thing in the morning," I explained, "and by early afternoon we should be on our way to New Mexico. Kerry thinks we can make it to Las Cruces by tomorrow night. There's supposed to be a really nice RV park there. Then it's on to Texas the next morning. The first few days we'll have longer drives because there's so much empty space in the desert. After that I only want to go about four hours a day."

"Do we have to travel over any mountains?" Mom asked with a worried look.

"No, Marge," Dad shot back, "we're gonna tunnel beneath them."

"Shit."

Mom's one-word comment caused more laughter. Everybody in the family knew that her lifelong fear of flying had mutated into a full-blown fear of anything moving faster than five miles per hour. She still drives a car on occasion but only takes right-hand turns at intersections, a tactic that greatly reduces her chances of being broadsided by a fully loaded Hummer traveling at a high rate of speed. The grocery store could be two minutes away, but if it means taking a left at the intersection my mother will instead go right at the light. She then drives a block in the opposite direction before turning right at the next corner. After driving for another block she takes a right at the next intersection, then proceeds to drive a block past the street she started on. When she arrives at the next corner she turns right, travels a block, then takes another right, goes another block, and hangs yet another right. Now she's back on the original street where the grocery store is located, though now it's ON THE RIGHT. It's also about twenty minutes later.

And that's best-case scenario. Add one-way streets, bridges, highway overpasses, or anything else that might alter the roadway geometry and what should have been a two-minute drive to the grocery turns into an overnight trip. As a passenger she is even more terrified, and therefore more annoying, as she screams, whimpers, and swears from her balled-up defensive posture on the floor of the backseat . . . before we leave the driveway.

I find this behavior odd because my mom was somewhat fearless as a younger woman, running out of the house to grab a baseball bat or to join us for a game of catch in the backyard. On one such occasion my brothers and I were throwing the ball around with my dad and one of his cohorts from work, a former minor-league pitcher who still had some hop on his fastball. My mother grabbed a mitt and the ex-pitcher let one go in her direction. It was dusk, and our grass-stained ball blended into the backdrop of trees and bushes. She didn't get her mitt up in time and the ball slammed into her face, leaving her with a broken nose and two black eyes. As soon as every-thing healed, however, she was back on the ball field smacking line drives into right field. Now she's terri-fied to make a right turn.

That's why I felt so happy seeing her laughing it up in the back of a gigantic RV, one day removed from rolling toward those steep mountain roads and beyond. Maybe the fears, anxieties, and loneliness of old age could be swept away by the joy of making one last family journey. Maybe my gripes about hav-ing to deal with those elderly issues could be erased by one final extravaganza of parent–child bonding. Matt, Margarita, Kerry, and Brendan said their good nights and left for the Winnebago parked behind us. My parents thanked me for rescuing them from the isolation of their rental home, then closed the door to their bedroom. I unfolded the convertible couch and prepared my bed for our first night of camping. I was feeling good, really good. I was also feeling hot, really hot. Walking over to the command center in the middle of the RV, I checked the thermostat. The little lever on the side had been jammed up into the high eighties. My mother wears sweaters in the sum-mer. This was her doing. It was going to be a battle.

Three

I opened one eye and looked at the portable digital clock balanced on the armrest of the sofa bed. It was 7:08 A.M. A gigantic pretrip worry had been erased. I had slept. Apparently, so had my parents. Either that or they were dead. Their bedroom door was still closed. There was no sign of movement. Distant thunder rumbled over the sound of steady rain. I reached over and hit the top of the small alarm clock and the rain stopped. The clock was also a sound machine. I lay my head back on the pillow and let my mind wander.

One of the selections on the sound machine was chirping crickets mixed with the occasional hoot of an owl. Why would anybody want crickets? I guess it's supposed to make you feel as if you're sleeping outside in the woods. Like I could fall asleep in the woods. Don't worry about the high-pitched whine, Mike, it's just a little mosquito trying to drop its West Nile payload into your ear canal. Oh, and don't pay any attention to the sound of those footsteps. Not every escapee from the nearby prison is a serial killer. Chances are he's just a white-collar felon and at worst you'll lose your life savings in his no-risk off-shore tax-shelter investment. Big deal. You can always move in with your parents.

**"Oh, it's nice to get up in the morning
in the good old summertime . . ."**

Dad was singing again. Lifting my head from the pillow I turned to see my father in mid-song standing in the bedroom doorway, dressed for the day. He wore shiny brown imitation alligator loafers, thick yellow athletic socks, powder-blue pants hemmed at the ankle, a navy-blue V-neck sweater, and a checkered shirt. Tying it all together was, yes, a tie. His singing continued:

**". . . but when the snow is snowing and it's
murky overhead,
it's nice to get up in the morning, but it's
better to lie in your bed."**

"Goooood morning, Mike," my father warbled. "I never slept so well in my life. Closed my eyes and bang, I was gone. Didn't move an inch all night."

"Why are you wearing a tie?" I asked.

"Oh, jeez, you have to look presentable, you have to . . ."

Before he could finish his sentence on the importance of wearing a tie when buying candy bars from heavily tattooed female convenience-store clerks standing behind rows of beef-jerky jars at highway filling stations, my mother shuffled out of the bedroom. She must not have read my dad's RV dress-code memo. She wore a tattered light-blue bathrobe, pink pjs, and white sweat socks. Her brownish-reddish hair was sleep-mashed to her head. She was a sight and she knew it.

"Oh my God, hide the children!" Dad shouted in mock horror.

"For better or for worse, Jack," Mom muttered.

"Sixty years, Margie, and I'm still waitin' for 'the better' to kick in."

Mom glanced at me and chuckled as she walked to the refrigerator. Dad picked up the sports section from yesterday's paper and sat down in one of the folding chairs by the dinette table. He was now whistling the Notre Dame fight song. I had slept in a T-shirt with the sleeves cut off and baggy exercise shorts. All I had to do was put on my socks and running shoes, grab a weighted jump rope from the overhead storage compartment, and I was ready for my exercise routine.

"Aren't you going to have breakfast?" Mom asked as she dropped two pieces of white bread into the toaster.

"No," I replied, "I have to do my sit-ups, run, and jump rope."

Eating a powdered doughnut, Dad looked up from the paper. "We used to jump rope at the Paterson Armory when we boxed as kids," he said. "How long do you go for?"

"I jump rope for thirty minutes, run three or four miles, then do my sit-ups. This is a light day, no weights. I'll be back in about an hour and a half."

"An hour and a half? That's ridiculous. You'll keel over. You'll . . ."

Mom's protesting was interrupted by a knock on the door. Pulling back the front curtain, I saw Kerry and Brendan standing outside the doorway. The Winnebago, with Matt at the wheel and Margarita in the passenger seat, was driving away.

"They're headed for the repair shop," Kerry said, climbing aboard. Brendan followed, his curly black hair alternately flattened and poofed up by the kind of hard sleep that only a nineteen-year-old boy can experience.

"Ahhhh, look who's here," Dad exclaimed, "Kerry and Brendan . . . what a treat!"

"You're father is nuts," grumbled Mom to Kerry

and Brendan as they looked through the cupboards for cereal. "He's fifty-six years old and he thinks he's a kid. What's he trying to prove? He's gonna have a heart attack."

It was a beautiful morning, and I started jumping rope off to the side of the Holiday Rambler. The Camping World store hadn't yet opened for the day and the parking lot was nearly empty. On the highway overpass above, the first wave of rush-hour traffic streaked by, whirring tires changing pitch as they came and went. Underneath the highway, a miniature tornado of dust blew toward a huge open field, where the world's longest freight train had finally clattered off into the distant mountains.

The RV's side window was open, and through the screen I heard everything that was being said. Much of it was about me.

"What's wrong with him?" questioned my mother. "Can't he just sit and relax once in a while?"

"Are you kidding me?" answered Kerry. "Sit and do nothing? He never just sits. He's gotta be doing at least two things at once."

"I'm surprised he hasn't figured out how to drive and do sit-ups at the same time," added Brendan. "He's always trying to get better at something, but he's kind of like those superheroes in the comics. His gift is his curse. He's super dedicated, but that makes him super annoying. Super impatient too. He reminds me of Lion-O."

"Thunder . . . Thunder . . . Thunder . . . Thundercats . . . Hoooo!" shouted Kerry, mimicking the opening cry from a cartoon series of the same name. **Thundercats** hadn't been seen in our house for at least fifteen years, yet Kerry and Brendan mimicked the opening theme song as if they'd just seen the cartoon that morning. Ask my children to quote anything from classic literature and all you get is stunned silence.

"I think I was about three when I started getting into **Thundercats**," said Brendan. "Dad reminds me of Lion-O because he has all these superpowers but the mind of a child."

"And he's bullheaded," whined my mother.

"I think he's freaked out about time," Kerry replied, "He's in middle age . . . actually he's beyond middle age, way past his peak, and he's trying to run back up the mountain but he keeps slipping back down, which just makes him run harder and slip more."

"The slippery side of the slope," my father chimed in. "We know it well, right, Marge? Eighty-seven . . . eighty-two . . . those are big numbers we're puttin' up."

"Old age sucks!" barked my mother. "You get wrinkles. Your hair gets thin. Everything goes to hell. My toenails look like Howard Hughes's. You can't cut them. They're like steel."

My kids laughed. Then my parents started laughing. I smiled and kept jumping.

Everybody in the family thinks that I push too hard. I don't think I push hard enough. When obstacles arise, my initial reflex is to look for a way around them. When failures occur, my automatic reaction is to figure out what went wrong and then try again. I wasn't born with that mindset; it came with practice. I screwed up plenty. Nothing came easy. Talent wasn't apparent. I knew early on that if I wanted to make something of myself, I would have to make it at **my** speed, piece by piece, inch by inch.

It's not about physical strength or moral character, because I can be as weak and as stupid as anybody out there. What it's about is resilience. And faith. Despite a mountain of shortcomings and no record of success, I somehow came to the conclusion, as a quiet, gawky fifteen-year-old high school kid, that I would make my mark in life by being creative. Who knows why? Without specific encouragement from anybody, especially in the classroom, where I flirted with failure throughout high school, the words "I want to be" were inexplicably replaced by the words "I will be." Where that inspiration came from remains a mystery.

In later years I realized that my weak intellect might have been a blessing in disguise. No situation was overanalyzed. No odds were calculated. It was all very basic. There had to be something good out there for me and there had to be a way to find it. Why wouldn't I be able to find it? The route is plainly marked. The directions are simple. Everybody knows the way. They also know that there are bumps along the way, and not everybody wants to feel those bumps.

"Just a little bump in the road, that's all it was!" exclaimed my father from the back of the Holiday Rambler. "Now everything's fixed up and we're ready to go, like nothing happened."

The Winnebago was idling next to us, its damaged side patched with white fiberglass. My credit card had taken a $3,000 hit, but I wasn't thinking about the money as I settled into the driver's seat and started the engine. Less than twenty-four hours earlier the whole journey seemed doomed, so I was just thankful that the RV was again up and running. To my right, Matt stood in the front stairwell of the Holiday Rambler fiddling with a camera. He had climbed aboard to photograph our second try at a launch and to help me with the long drive to New Mexico. Kerry and Margarita would trade shifts at the wheel of the Winnebago while Brendan, too young to legally drive a rental vehicle, would hop between RVs, doing odd jobs along the way. The open road awaited us. Only one thing held us back.

"Son of a bitch."

It was my mother, talking to herself as she rooted through her big, baglike purse. Whatever she was looking for wasn't there, so she started pulling the cushions off the sofa bed.

"Shit," she mumbled after finding nothing but a ballpoint pen and a gum wrapper. A second later she was on her hands and knees, trying to peer beneath the sofa bed's metal frame.

"Marge," pleaded my father, "we can't move until you sit down. What the hell are you looking for?"

"I can't find my goddamn holy card," she muttered.

Matt stifled a laugh. You don't often hear the words "holy card" and "goddamn" strung together in the same sentence.

"What holy card?" I asked.

"My Mother Teresa holy card," she answered, crawling on the floor. "She's a saint. She's gonna get me there and get me home. Now where the hell is she?"

"Check your sleeve," I suggested, knowing how my mother likes to jam balls of Kleenex and other objects up the sleeves of her sweaters.

"Oh, for heaven's sakes. There she is!" Mom exclaimed in a relieved voice. "Okay, now we can go."

It was the middle of the afternoon. Traffic was light as we drove our two RVs through Mesa's streets looking for the highway entrance. I was feeling a bit more comfortable behind the wheel, not that Mom seemed to notice. She was sitting—actually, more like crouching—on the edge of the sofa, her hands gripping the armrests, her white-sneakered feet screwing into the carpet for support. The top of Mother Teresa's head, swaddled in Kleenex, peeked from her sleeve. What a comfort to know that my mom had done everything humanly possible to brace herself for the fiery head-on collision that she fully expected—everything except buckle her seat belt.

On the opposite side of the RV, Dad whistled "It's a Grand Old Flag" while eating another doughnut and reading **USA Today.** The newspaper was spread over the dinette table. My father sat in a portable wooden folding chair. A sticker on the wall read "This seat not for occupancy while vehicle is in motion." Every few minutes, for no apparent reason, he looked up and grinned. Seeing his chair skitter and hop with each bump in the road caused me to repeatedly yell out a warning for him to move to a different seat. He just nodded, flashed another smile, and stayed put. Mom's right; he does need a wad of gum.

I was thankful that my oldest son, Matt, was riding along in the passenger seat next to me. Tall and thin, Matt.

with dark wavy hair and a ready smile, he was always polite, patient, and considerate. He would do anything to help out. With a long drive ahead of us, it was nice to know that he could take the reins now and then. But could he take the bombardment? Was he strong enough to sit through the never-ending volley of verbal rockets? What I needed, more than a driver, was a decoy, someone to draw the conversational fire away from me. Cruising across an America filled with mega-malls, superstores, franchised food joints, and other such monuments to low wages and high profits would undoubtedly provoke my father into launching a whole new barrage of the same old sermons about the little man getting an ass-whipping. That's when I needed Matt to activate the missile shield and change the subject.

"Did you see that hotdog?" exclaimed my father from the back of the RV. We were now on the freeway and a pickup truck had just zoomed by on the left. The driver had worn his baseball hat backward. My old man hates that.

"Catchers and welders, those are the only people who should wear their hats like that. If you're gonna put on a hat, put it on right." Dad shook his head, pausing for a second—just a second. "That guy probably saw some movie star wearing it like that and now he's doing the same. Of course, that guy's driving a beat-up truck and the movie star—who probably couldn't catch a beach ball if I threw it to him—works two months a year and makes ten million bucks. Nobody's worth that kind of money, not when hard-working people can't make enough money to feed their family. The system is out of whack, the rich are getting richer and . . ."

This is where I had hoped Matt would jump in and derail the conversation before it got rolling. But it was too late. Dad's lecture train, "The Bleeding Heart Limited," had left the station and was gaining speed. Someone had to take drastic action, and that someone was supposed to have been Matt. I wanted to turn and give him The Look, but we were in a construction zone and I couldn't take my eyes off the road. Why wasn't he responding? Why wasn't Matt doing his job?

"Mike, you've got one hand on the wheel!"

My dad's runaway train had just picked up its first passenger: my mom.

"And what the hell are you doing with the other hand?" she moaned. "Are you playing a guitar or something? God save us."

"It's not a guitar," I replied, "it's a little wooden thing I strap around my waist. It's got five strings on it. I wear it when I drive so I can practice my banjo rolls."

Dad laughed. "Who the hell other than Mike Leonard would drive a van loaded with valuable cargo, his mother and father, while strumming a guitar with nothin' coming out of it?"

"It's not a guitar," I repeated. "It's not supposed to sound like music. I'm just working on my finger movements."

"Quit asking him questions, Jack!" cried my mother. "Now he's talking, driving, and playing the guitar at the same time. And we're on the goddamn freeway. Slow down! I can't take this."

Where the hell was Matt? Taking a chance, I glanced quickly to my right. Matt stared out the side window. Wearing earphones, holding an iPod in his left hand. My copilot had already bailed on me.

"Hey Mike." It was Dad's voice again. "Remember when you and Cathy moved to Phoenix? You were jammed into that little car with all the clothes and wedding presents. Too bad you couldn't have traveled across the country in a big bus like this."

"How's Cathy doing?" Mom interjected, her voice still tense with fear.

"She's good. I talked with her this morning. She wishes she could be riding along, but with the baby due in a month she wanted to stay close to Meg and Jamie."

"Well, Meg's contributing to society," said my father. "There was a great story in World War II, a person in the Navy asking his commanding officer for leave because his wife was having a baby and they refused his leave, and the note on it was 'You were there for the laying of the keel and you don't have to be there for the launching.' Get it? New ships."

"You **should** be there," said my mom in a serious voice as she looked out the window. "First babies are tough. You don't know what you're up against."

My parents got married in a full-blown church ceremony forty-eight hours after announcing their engagement. They had only two days to buy rings, recruit the wedding party, pick out dresses, send invitations, choose flowers, secure a church, purchase a cake, and plan a reception for 150 people. It was the summer of 1943. Wartime. My father's Navy ship was set to sail out of New York Harbor within a week. Why wait?

A wartime wedding in July 1943.

There was something else that caused my mother to act so quickly. Fragments of information pieced together through the years clued me in to a darker set of motives that might have compelled her to get married in such a rush. I had a feeling that something wasn't right in the house where my mom grew up. That something, I guessed, was her father. She never talked about George.

To us.

Good spies, however, hear things.

It would be nighttime. Lights off in our bedrooms. All quiet on the little-boy front. That's when my brothers and I would noiselessly crawl out of our beds, imagining that we were brave soldiers risking our lives by sneaking across enemy lines to eavesdrop on the hostile forces. Across the bedroom carpet we would slink, then out into the hall and over to the second-floor banister, carefully avoiding the minefield of creaky boards. Peeking between the narrowly spaced spindles, we could see a section of the living room where my parents would sometimes sit and talk about things they didn't want us to hear.

Like things about George.

Cracking the language code of marital life was a difficult challenge for little-boy spies. Certain words, however, sunk in. "Cruel" was one of those words. Then one night, on a particularly dangerous mission after my parents had made a big deal out of getting us to bed early, we crawled to our posts and overheard something startling. George was dead. My mom's voice was shaky, but we could pick up bits and pieces of her conversation. Something about her mother having no place to live, about George and the horse track, about money in the bank disappearing. We crawled back to our base camp, climbed safely into our beds, and lay there in silence, wondering what it all meant.

A few weeks later my brothers and I rode with my

Margaret Hattersley gets a happy welcome from her grandsons Mike, Jack, and Tim.

father to the train station in Chicago. We stayed in the backseat of the car while Dad stood on the sidewalk outside the station doorway. A crowd of people came out followed by a white-haired woman in a blue polka-dot dress. She carried one suitcase. My father hugged her and she started to cry. Then Dad pointed toward our car and the white-haired lady looked in our direction and smiled. That's the day my grandmother moved in. She would stay with us until she died, twenty-five years later.

"Jeez, I'd like to have that head full of nickels," cracked my father, peering out from under the huge L.A. Dodgers baseball cap that Brendan had dropped on his head. "You got some noggin. What size?"

"I think I'm a size eight." Brendan took the cap back from my father and put it on his own head . . . backward.

"Oh, not you too," Dad moaned.

The RVs were parked side by side in the middle of an open patch of desert somewhere in southern Arizona. We had pulled off the highway to eat a late lunch and had gathered in the Holiday Rambler.

"That's a Leonard trait," I said, "big heads."

"And no brains," cracked Mom. "Except for Kevin. Where the hell did he come from, anyhow?"

"Hey Mike," called out Dad, "when you had your first serious accident and cracked your head in that

store . . . it was on the corner of a glass counter-
top . . . My father had come for a visit from New Jersey and God, he was so upset. You were about two
years old and were bleeding and he was shaking like
a leaf but he was so kind in picking you up and taking care of you. He was a kind man. It was the Mar-
shall Field's store, wasn't it, Marge?"

"No, it was Weiboldt's. We went there to get . . ."

In the middle of her answer Dad leaped to his feet.
The reminiscing had unearthed another long-buried
musical number. He began singing:

> **"Oh, I used to work in Chicago at the Field's**
> > **Department Store,**
> **I used to work in Chicago, I did but I don't**
> > **anymore.**
> **A lady came in for some garters, I asked her**
> > **what kind she wore,**
> **'Rubber,' she said, rubber I did, I don't**
> > **work there anymore."**

Once again, the RV was rocked by laughter.

"Where do these songs come from?" sputtered
Margarita.

"I don't know," Dad responded as he sat back down
in the easy chair. "Just stuff I remember from growing
up. There was always music in our house. My uncle
Johnny—Johnny Smith, my mother's brother—lived
with us for a lot of years and he sang and danced and

played the fiddle and the tin whistle and oh, he could do anything. Tough too. Jeez, could he fight. All-Ireland football player from Cavan . . . Big guy, wore these white turtleneck Irish sweaters, curly black hair, handsome. I idolized him when I was a kid. One time my father came home after having one too many at the bar and you could tell that somebody'd popped him. His nose was bloody and he was woozy. We were eating dinner and my mother was upset. I was about ten years old and Johnny was sitting right across from my older sister and me. He kept chewing his food, didn't say anything. A few minutes later he excused himself, got up from the table, put on his cap, and started for the front door. My mom said, 'Johnny, where ya goin'?' He answered, 'Just out for a bit of walk, Annie.' I heard later that he went back to the bar and cleaned the place out."

"Did your dad drink a lot?" Matt asked.

"Not a lot. He always worked, always got up early, but every now and then he would go on a bit of a bender. It worried my mom because she was afraid he might lose his job. I didn't like to see her upset, so I promised her that I'd never drink and I never have. Back then times were tough and good jobs were hard to come by. My dad worked for the phone company. Started out diggin' ditches and eventually became a supervisor. Hard worker. Dependable. Smart too, but never got past the second grade."

My dad took a bite from his ham sandwich. I had

A young Tom Leonard.

left the front door open and a soft desert breeze, mixed with the muffled sound of the distant freeway traffic, drifted in.

"My father was nineteen when he got on the boat and came to America. He was just a farm kid from County Sligo with ten bucks in his pocket, stuck in the lowest section of a crummy boat with a bunch of other scared and lonely kids just like him. Six days at sea and he never got out from below deck to see the ocean. There was no work in Ireland. The country just emptied out its young people. Mike, imagine how heartsick you'd be, knowing that Brendan would be leaving in a few months and you'd never see him again. Imagine how sad you'd be when the time got short and he started gathering up his belongings and packing them into a suitcase. You'd be looking at his young face, his curly hair, his hands, trying to remember every detail. They didn't have any photographs. They had no money for paintings.

"Brendan, think of what it must have been like for people your age, leaving your home and your family. That's why so many of those Irish songs are sad—'Danny Boy,' 'Galway Bay.' My father was like Brendan, a teenage boy, when he walked away from their little farmhouse in Tubbercurry. It was the last time he saw his mother and father. I don't know how he did that. I couldn't. It was the same with my mother. She left County Cavan and met my father in America."

"Kevin showed me the passenger list from the ship your dad was on," I said. My younger brother Kevin is an archivist for Northwestern University and the keeper of family records. "He told me that anybody can get that stuff on the Ellis Island website. Just put in the name and the approximate date and up comes a picture of the ship and a list of passengers, their ages, how much money they had with them, stuff like that. Tom Leonard was on a ship called **The Oceanic** with seventeen hundred other people on their way to America. I was amazed at the ages of the passengers—Frank Gaffney, eighteen; Annie Farrell, fifteen; Patrick Mulcahy, twenty. Those kinds of names, all young, all leaving home."

Brendan turned to my mother. "Hey Moose, did your parents come over like that?"

"My grandparents did," said Mom. "My grandmother's name was Bridget O'Halloran. She came from Cork and married a man named Martin Curley from Roscommon. He ran Curley's Tavern in Paterson. It was a real nice place. My mother's name was Margaret Curley, but then she got married and it became Margaret Hattersley."

Mom took a sip from her water bottle and looked out the window. The brief silence was broken by my father's voice.

"Your mother was the nicest woman who ever stepped on the face of this earth. Never complained. And so pretty."

"But what about your dad?" Brendan asked. "I never hear about him. What was his name again?"

"George," answered my mother, still looking out the window. "He came from England."

That's all she said.

"Let's get moving." I announced. "We've still got a ways to go before we hit Las Cruces."

Our caravan of two pulled onto the highway and headed for the mountains of New Mexico while my mind headed back to the mention of that name— Bridget O'Halloran. I didn't know much about my great-grandmother. She had died in New Jersey at the age of forty. Her daughter, my grandmother, moved into our house when I was six years old, and my father was right in calling her the nicest woman on earth. She never seemed to be in a bad mood and had a great sense of humor—a necessary survival trait in the goofy Leonard household.

When my youngest brother, Kevin, was born two months premature, my grandmother got him through a difficult early childhood. He wasn't expected to live and was sickly as a young boy. My parents had their hands full with the three of us, so Kevin became my grandmother's child. She was constantly at his side, reading to him, talking to him, keeping him out of harm's way when our mischievous minds went into overdrive. That's why Kevin is so smart. That's why he got good grades in school. My brothers and I would be standing on chairs in the bathroom, burping and pouring pots of water into the toilet to see who could best replicate the sound of a violently vomiting child, while Kevin and my grandmother sat in the upstairs den reading "Hansel and Gretel."

As my grandmother grew older she would occasionally have one too many glasses of wine and get dizzy. One summer evening when I was about thirteen years old, I looked out the kitchen window and saw her on the ground in the backyard. She had gone outside to tidy things up and had fallen. I watched as she tried to get back on her feet, only to keep falling back down. Mom and Dad weren't home, so I ran outside and helped her up. Woozy from wine, she couldn't walk, even with my help. Cradling her in my arms like a baby, I struggled to carry her toward the house. My grandmother's room was on the third floor and I was small for my age, but there was nobody around to help. Across the backyard we went, through the small kitchen, the hallway, up one flight of stairs and then another. The steps to her room

My grandmother and me.

were steep and narrow, and I was straining mightily just to hold on. My grandmother never spoke as we slowly made our way up the stairs, but with her head in the crook of my left arm I couldn't avoid looking at her face and seeing an expression of sorrow—sorrow for being in that condition, sorrow for being a burden to me, and sorrow for something else. I finally made it to her bed, and after I put her down she looked up at me and in a quiet voice said, "I've had a hard life."

My grandmother lived with my parents until she died at the age of eighty-six. I have home movies that show her playfully feeling Cathy's big stomach just days before Matt was born. Taking those movies, then splicing together the worthwhile scenes and putting them to music, was my creative outlet. It was also the only method I knew to slow down the time that seemed to speed by. But it came at a cost. High-quality movies demand a high-priced camera plus a projector, and that's what I emptied my bank account to buy ten months before Cathy and I were married. It was a Super 8 film system, the format of choice prior to the introduction of videotape. The film, sold in little three-and-a-half-minute spools, was also expensive, as was the process of having it developed at a photo lab. It became an issue.

During the first eight years of our marriage I often changed occupations, trying to keep a roof overhead while searching for the creative destiny that awaited

Mike and Cathy move to Phoenix.
Babies follow soon afterward.

me. The interim jobs were often menial and the pay
low. With Cathy staying home to care for our first
three children, it was up to me to make ends
meet . . . and to make movies. I had to make movies.
The baby's first bath, the baby's first solid meal, the
baby's first steps—moments that we couldn't let pass
were recorded on film that we couldn't afford. As the
children grew, so did the scope of the movies, edited
into short films that told the story of our simple but
happy life. In the late 1970s, a sample reel of those

home movies led to a job in television, which leads me now to Bridget O'Halloran.

During college I had a summer job working construction on Chicago's Lake Shore Drive. My parents had moved to Arizona, so my summertime residence was a YMCA not far from Cathy's house. The room had no phone, no toilet, and no sink, but it didn't matter. The rent was only fourteen bucks a week, which allowed me to save more money for an engagement ring. My plan was to work right up until the last weekend of the summer, deposit the paycheck on Friday, buy the ring on Saturday, propose on Sunday, and head back east for college early Monday morning. By summer's end I had a thousand dollars in the bank. Eight hundred was earmarked for the ring.

After my last day of work, I called my parents from a YMCA pay phone to announce that I was going to buy a ring the following afternoon and propose to Cathy that weekend. At one point in the conversation, Dad handed the phone to my grandmother, who told me, out of the blue, that she had been saving her mother's ring for this occasion. Her words caught me by surprise. I had worked all summer to save enough money for an engagement ring and now my grandmother was offering to **give** me a ring—her mother's ring—Bridget O'Halloran from County Cork. When my father got back on the phone, I told him how appreciative I was and then explained the problem with the gift.

It was late Friday afternoon and I was going to propose to Cathy on Sunday, then leave for school on Monday. How could I get the ring in time? There was no FedEx in 1969. Dad said that he would try to think of something and told me to stay near a phone on Saturday. The next morning he called me at Cathy's house with instructions to go to O'Hare that afternoon. A plane from Phoenix would be arriving at 4:00 P.M. I was to wait in the arrival lounge. The ring would be delivered.

What my father did couldn't be done today. He took Bridget O'Halloran's ring to Sky Harbor Airport in Phoenix and because there were no security checkpoints in those days, simply walked to the departure lounge of a Chicago-bound flight and waited for the flight attendants to show up. When they did, my dad approached one of the women and asked, "Could you deliver this ring to my son?" When she agreed my dad handed her the diamond ring, explained that I would be waiting at the arrival gate in Chicago, and left. He never asked the flight attendant's name.

The plane landed on time. The passengers dispersed, leaving me standing there alone. A flight attendant peered out from the jet bridge, walked over to me slowly, and said, "You must be the boy." I nodded my head. Out of her pocket came a folded-up napkin, and out of that napkin came a diamond ring. She placed the ring in my hand, gave me a hug, and said, "Have a wonderful life." Then she walked away.

A diamond ring once worn by an Irish immigrant who trusted fate by sailing off to an unknown land had just sailed across America in the trusted hands of an unknown woman. A day later I gave that same diamond ring to a pretty girl who believed me when I said that I would find my place in the world, and after eight long years of struggle, I did find my place by showing home movies on the wall of a news director's office. Those movies came from a camera that I bought in Chicago on the weekend of my engagement. The movie camera cost eight hundred dollars—the eight hundred dollars left in my bank account thanks to the gift of Bridget O'Halloran's ring.

Four

"Where the hell is he?"

The morning sun shone brightly on the tidy rows of RVs at the KOA campsite in Las Cruces, New Mexico. I squinted through the windshield mumbling to myself. My father knew we wanted to get a jump on the day's travels, but his desperate need to suck the conversational blood from a fresh victim must have been too much to bear, and now he was gone. I had feared this might happen, because last night's late arrival had deprived Dad of prime talk time. When dawn broke, so did he.

"He's got somebody cornered, some sucker who doesn't know what hit him," groused my mother, peering out the side window. "It's pathetic. Honk the horn."

"I don't want to wake the other campers," I replied, "and besides . . . Wait, there he is, between those two RVs. He's got his hand on that man's arm. Oh crap, he's not letting go."

My mother hustled to the front of the RV to see for herself.

"It's a sickness. I swear to God, it's a sickness," she moaned. "Damn it!"

With that, my mother scooted past me and leaned on the center of the steering wheel. A long, low foghorn blast shattered the morning calm. My father's head quickly swiveled in our direction . . . then back to the man . . . then back to us. His body language conveyed a mixture of fear and longing. Fear made him wave a hurried good-bye to the confused fellow and take a few steps toward us. Longing stopped him in his tracks and jerked his body back into position for another run at the defenseless camper. Three or four seconds passed with Dad caught in a form of suspended animation . . . minus, that is, the suspense.

"Oh, he's not done," Mom groaned, "not by a long shot. He'll go back. Watch."

Sure enough, my father swooped back in for the kill. We've seen it happen a million times and it drives us crazy. It's not his talking that's the problem, because if you can distract him from the subject of the common man suffering yet another undeserved butt-whipping, his conversations are actually interesting.

Getting him to end the conversation, however, is another story . . . another long story . . . another long story without an end. The man simply cannot bring himself to say good-bye.

"Hell with it," Mom proclaimed, throwing her hands up in frustration. "Leave him here. He can hitchhike to Texas."

My father was eventually pulled away from the carcass and escorted back to the RV. It was about 11:00 A.M. when we finally rolled out of the campsite and headed toward the other side of the freeway, where a huge Wal-Mart sign loomed above a shopping center. The crash of the Winnebago at the start of our journey had robbed us of the opportunity to buy supplies in Arizona, so this was a stop we thought necessary. My father disagreed.

"I'm not going in."

He sat in the Holiday Rambler's swiveling lounge chair with his arms folded defiantly. An untamed shock of hair sprouted from one side of his head. He had lost his comb. Wal-Mart sells combs. But Dad wasn't buying.

"It's a philosophical matter," he decreed. "Big companies are taking over the world. The little ma-and-pa stores are getting eaten alive."

"But it's just a comb," I said.

"I'm taking a stand," answered my father. "They're not getting my money."

"Holy shit!" I gasped sarcastically. "Do you know

what the loss of that sixty cents is going to do to their stock price tomorrow? Quick, somebody call Martha Stewart!"

"That's another thing," he railed, "rich people like her get all the stock tips. That's why the little guy on the street can't make money on the market. It's not the way it should . . ."

"It was a joke!" I sighed. "Listen, I have to go in and buy a bunch of stuff. I'll be back in about a half hour."

"Don't worry about me," my father replied righteously. "I'll be fine here all by myself. Say, Mike, while you're in there could you get me a candy bar?"

The second day's drive was another long one. We had to get through vast uninhabited sections of land on this leg of the journey, so we didn't plan any sightseeing stops. The wild card in the deal was, of course, my mother. All bets were off on how she would react going through the mountains of New Mexico. As we got rolling, though, the bookies were shocked by her surprisingly muted performance in the early going. They say it was mind over matter, although some have whispered that it might actually have been wine over mind over matter. Who cares? She was quiet. She was also bent in a sideways U for most of the day, head in hands, eyes locked onto her sneakers.

The mountain views were incredible. But Mom wasn't looking, and Dad seemed oddly unimpressed.

His tepid reaction to the spectacular scenery confused me. This part of the country was new to my
parents and I had expected more of a response, especially from Dad. Then, as we approached the outskirts of El Paso, he suddenly perked up, craning his
head toward the side window for a better view of
whatever it was that had caught his interest. A natural wonder? An old fort? An eagle? No.

"Hey Marge . . . look, Office Depot!"

"Where?" Now my mother couldn't get enough of
the scenery. "Oh, yeah. Wow!"

Since leaving Phoenix we had seen a desert in
bloom, an awe-inspiring mountain range, a spectacular rainbow, a glorious sunset . . . and not a word
from either of them. Nothing. Then up pops a damn
Office Depot sign and my parents react as if they'd
just come upon Elvis and Jackie O skipping hand in
hand across the north rim of the Grand Canyon . . .
better yet, the north rim of a Contempo Casuals
parking lot.

"Jack, quick, on the right . . . Pottery Barn!"

"I can't see it, Marge . . . Oh, now I do . . . isn't
that something? And look down the street . . . Food
Lion."

"Damn!" my mother exclaimed. "I missed it."

But she didn't miss Linens-n-Things or Costco or
White Hen or Radio Shack or Motel 6 . . . even
Burger King, for God's sake! The interior of the Holiday Rambler crackled with excitement as we made
our way through the heavily franchised outskirts of

El Paso. Once the last Fashion Bug had faded from view, however, the crackle turned soggy as we cruised east along a breathtakingly beautiful stretch of Highway 10. Near the tiny west Texas town of Van Horn, the mood briefly spiked when a Pizza Hut sign was spotted. It quickly plunged again when the scenery improved.

Were they always like this? I couldn't ask Matt, my son and RV traveling partner; he was too many generations removed from the answer. Besides, the sheer magnitude of bizarreness exhibited by the sightseeing episode had driven him back into the comforting womb of his iPod. This was my baby to wrestle. And it was one big-ass crazy baby swaddled in worrisome questions about genetics. If my parents are indeed crazy, where does that leave me? For starters, it left me wondering about my childhood.

It was the 1950s. Dogs weren't leashed. Kids weren't scheduled. A summer day would dawn in our small Midwestern town and out the front doors boys and beasts flew. No structure. No plan. I was the second-oldest of four mischievous boys, and our daily mission was to make something out of nothing. Every now and then, that something exploded.

From the earliest age I struggled in school. I could have had a learning disability, but we didn't know about that stuff back then. In our Catholic grammar school there were no remedial classes, no accelerated learning programs, no individualized anything. We were all lumped together, the bright lights and the dim bulbs. And it was a huge lump: fifty-some kids per classroom, one overworked nun, and a much simpler formula for categorizing students of different abilities:

Dyslexic = Dope
Motor Skills Disorder = Spaz

Mike hits the books. The books hit back. Hard.

Each category, of course, had divisions. The hard-core stupids, the big kids with the puzzled expressions, were placed in the Lower Dope classification. Ten-year-old third-graders always have a size advantage. Larry was one of those kids. I'm not using his real name, because I don't want him tracking me down. I fear yet another headlock. Larry once head-locked me for an entire second-grade lunch period; only the threadbare fabric of a flannel shirt separated his armpit from my nose. That was my first encounter with B.O. Who has B.O. in the primary grades? Serial flunkies like Larry do. That's why I never sat next to him in the school cafeteria. That and his streak of spilling a carton of milk every day from kindergarten to eighth grade. (See Motor Skills Disorder.)

The marginally stupid like me were slotted in the Upper Dope division—a rank filled mostly by mischief-makers. We could instantly calculate the angle, velocity, and speed needed by a thrown snow-ball to arc across a school playground and intersect with a walking teacher's hat—yet would also sit in slack-jawed bafflement when asked how many times six goes into thirty, which we all know is . . . well, we all know. How did I fall into that life of academic ineptitude?

Basically, I fell.

School had let out in my small hometown of Glencoe, Illinois, and a few of us were standing on a street corner seeing how many wads of bubble gum we could jam into the pay-phone coin-return compartment. That's what third-graders did in the Pre-Superchild Era. We didn't have soccer practice, voice lessons, or college-entrance-exam prep sessions. So we invented things to do, like seeing who could spit the farthest or hold his breath the longest. Spitting was all technique, never my strong suit in anything. Breath holding, however, was pure determination, my one true talent.

Bending my knees for support, I gulped as much air as my little lungs would hold, gritted my teeth, sealed my lips, and held my breath. And held my breath. And held my breath. Then I passed out, crashing forehead first onto the concrete curb. When I regained consciousness, my view of the world had been permanently altered. Something inside my head got jarred loose or fused shut. The prize for my victory was to be a bag of Malted Milk Balls. What I got instead was a lifetime of flunked exams, exorbitantly miscalculated restaurant tips, and shocking memory lapses.

The immediate fallout, though, was purely physical. I threw up, then tumbled sideways into a parked car and fell back down. The world was a turntable, the old-school kind, spinning fast at 78 rpm. Crawling to a parking meter, I grabbed the pole for support, pulled myself up, and climbed onto my fat-tired bike. Our house was straight down the street, two blocks away. I began to pedal, but the sidewalk tilted and everything around me swirled. I crashed into a stone water fountain, a wooden fence, a clump of bushes, and finally a tree. Then everything went black. When I woke up I was strapped to a hospital bed. The room revolved around me. A doctor tapped his finger against my bandaged forehead and a vibrating shock wave rippled through my brain. I had suffered a massive concussion. Three days in the hospital were followed by three more days of bed rest at home. No television, no comic books, no rapid movement or jarring physical activity was allowed.

I'm not good with boredom. By Day Three I was imagining that my fur Davey Crockett hat was singing "Zippity Do Dah" to a lamp in the corner of my bedroom, so I begged my mom to let me walk to the park and back. The park was at the end of the block, only six houses down the street from us. It was early afternoon and the neighborhood kids were still in school, so the danger level seemed low. My mother reluctantly agreed to let me go, but the terms of her pardon were strict: Walk to the park and walk back. Don't go on the swings. Don't climb any trees. No running. No jungle gym. No slide. No teeter-totter. Be home in ten minutes.

I had a headache and my eyes hurt in the bright sunlight, but it still felt good being out of the house. Halfway down the block I ran into my best friend, Ricky Leslie, sprung from public school early because of a teacher's meeting.

"Hey Mike," Ricky asked with his usual enthusiasm, "do you want to go to see Bobby and Buddy?"

"Sure," I answered without hesitation.

Bobby and his younger brother Buddy lived in the middle of our block. The neighborhood was filled with kids, mostly boys possessing the same kind of knuckleheaded tendencies that the Leonards so valued. Bobby and Buddy were above-average nutty, and down to their basement we went. As usual, there was nothing to do, so we invented a hybrid game of indoor horseless polo hockey. I was the goalie. The contest wasn't a minute old before I was struck in the forehead by a wooden croquet ball.

Reservations booked, Mr. Leonard. Your permanent seat in the Upper Dope section has been confirmed.

I don't recall how Mom greeted me when I walked back into the house with a dopey look and swollen forehead. Maybe the impact of the croquet ball shut down another branch of my memory bank, deleting all records of her reaction. Or maybe I don't remember her reaction because she didn't have one. Maybe she just shrugged it off, as other mothers once did when the bumpy road through childhood actually did get bumpy. Kids fell out of trees, got hit in the head with rocks, and were bit by dogs, and nobody raised a stink.

When I was about ten, I brought my younger brother Kevin and his friend Richard to a park and introduced them to the joys of flaming plastic. Earlier backyard research had led to the astounding discovery that a lighted match could transform a yellow plastic Wiffle Ball bat into a World War II bomber, spewing a steady stream of tiny, melted plastic fireballs. With Kevin and Richard looking on, I lit the top of the bat and started bombing a supply train of ants. At one point I glanced back at the boys and saw their expressions quickly turn from awe to horror. In my excitement I had forgotten to check the rate of burn. The only part of the bat that wasn't on fire was the six-inch, black taped handle. Hoping that a rush of air would extinguish the blaze, I swung the bat with all my might. A tennis ball–size chunk of flaming plastic flew off the end of the bat. Red warning lights flashed and sirens wailed at mission control. The flaming missile was headed right for Richard's face.

It's a strange feeling to look into the incredulous eyes of a screaming five-year-old, his right cheek on fire, and know that you are to blame. It's also weird, and extremely troubling, to see that same screaming little boy running home, black smoke trailing behind his head, knowing that within minutes his parents would be stomping down your driveway, smoking kid in tow as evidence, demanding some kind of horrible punishment for the missile launch commander. I went home, sat on my bed, and waited for the doorbell to ring. It never rang. Nothing was ever mentioned. Through the years I've often wondered what kind of conversation took place after Richard burst through the front door of his house.

Flaming Richard: "Mom! Mom! My face is on fire."

Flaming Richard's Mom: "Calm down, Richard. What happened?"

Flaming Richard: "Mike's bat bomber shot a missile into my face."

Flaming Richard's Mom: "Here, let me put the fire out."

(Hissing sound from wet kitchen sponge coming in contact with smoking cheek.)

Flaming Richard: "Thanks, Mom. Can I go back to Mike's house?"

Flaming Richard's Mom: "Sure, but not right now. We're about to have dinner. Your favorite: beenie weenie."

Flaming Richard: "Yipee!"

We liked beenie weenie too. And SpaghettiO's. And Spam. And anything else that could be canned, frozen, or somehow chemically altered to earn the shelf-life marking "Eat Before the Apocalypse." Ours was the kitchen where taste went to die. My mother hated to cook and we didn't care. Dinnertime was

like an Indianapolis 500 pit stop. Race in, fuel up,
race out.

Our spacious kitchen counter. Also
pictured—Inky, the insane dog.

The seating arrangement was odd but understandable. My parents, seeking temporary solace, re-
treated to their bunker in the dining room. Jack,
Timmy, and I sat crammed together at a three-foot-
long kitchen counter wedged between a red-hot
burner on the stove and the wall. Kevin dined with
our grandmother off TV trays in the upstairs den,
apparently in the belief that watching television over

dinner every night would help him unwind from another trying day as our personal laboratory animal.

It was all in the interest of science. How else could we test the suction-tip strength of a new dart gun without using Kevin's large forehead for a target? In what other way could we accurately determine the maximum length of a static-electricity lightning bolt without scraping our woolen socks across a houseful of cheap carpet, then converging, index fingers extended toward Kevin's moist nose?

"La Quinta Inn, Marge!"

My father's call from the Holiday Rambler's lounge chair jolted me back to the present. The sudden cluster of motel signs along Highway 10 signaled the start of our approach into the Fort Stockton area. The high desert terrain of west Texas had flattened out and the brownish yellow ground cover looked dull in the fading sunlight. Our home for the night, the Fort Stockton KOA campground was just off the highway, its entrance marked by a fiberglass cowboy with a plaque that read "Land of the Free."

The land wasn't free. It never is. Camping slots in RV parks vary in price depending on location, amenities, and time of year. The Fort Stockton KOA (Kampgrounds of America) charged us (Kharged us) about twenty bucks per vehicle per night, which is about what we figured we'd pay at the most of the other places. You can use the RV generator and camp

for free in a Wal-Mart parking lot or on the side of
some road, but that means refilling the propane and
water tanks at a faster pace, so it's cheaper to stay at
the parks and use the provided hookups for water and
electricity. Most camps also offer showers and coin-
operated laundry machines. Some even have pools,
hot tubs, recreational centers, and supply stores.

The Fort Stockton KOA was a mid-level campsite.
The outdoor pool and hot tub were shut down for
the winter. Attendance was sparse. Something told
me that Pecos County, Texas, in late February wasn't
included on many of the travel magazine "Hot Spot"
lists. We didn't care. We were there to sleep. And to
jerk my dad's chain.

Once again, we all gathered in the Holiday Rambler for an easy dinner of pasta and assorted Lean
Cuisine entrées. Mom and Dad sat side by side at the
kitchen table, facing the front of the RV. While the
meals were being prepared, Brendan sidled over to
me, opened his coat to shield the hidden object from
my parents, and showed me the DVD. It was **AC/DC
Live at Donington.** My father hadn't ranted in a
while, and nothing gets him going better than some
good headbanging music. Brendan turned on the flat-
screen TV that was situated above the front windshield, put the DVD into the player, and cranked the
volume.

My parents stared in horror while the music blared
and a long-haired, shirtless guitar player skipped

across the concert stage in his velvety English school-
boy shorts. The look on Dad's face was one of shock
mixed with puzzlement mixed with despair garnished
with a twist of anger. It was as if **Dateline NBC** had
just aired exclusive surveillance video of St. Patrick
wearing a strapless evening gown. We figured one
song would be enough to get my father going, and we
figured right.

"They're crazy," he muttered as soon as the TV
was turned off. "They're nuts. That's what the world
is coming to."

"What do you call that group?" my mother asked.

"AC/DC," Brendan answered.

"In my day, people tried to keep that stuff quiet,"
Dad fumed. "Bing Crosby could come out and
sing . . ."

"Bing Crosby was a drunk!" shouted Mom, to
hysterical laughter from the rest of us.

This was a bonus. Not only had we succeeded in
getting my father to blow a circuit, we had also managed to provoke a decent skirmish between the two.

"Bing Crosby was great!" my father shouted back.

"He was awful," countered my mother. "He was
never home with his family."

"What was he supposed to do?" argued my dad,
"bring them with him? He was entertaining; that's
how they were living."

"Bullshit!" my mother shot back. "He was playing
golf at Pebble Beach."

That last verbal punch seemed to knock my father off his fight plan. He started backpedaling.

"Well," he sighed, "Bing was a great entertainer. And I could understand the words to his songs."

The fight had gone out him. His only chance now was to try and influence the judges with a fancy flourish at the end. That's why he started singing.

"Toooora looora looora . . ."

"Toora loora, my ass!" yelled my mother.

And that's all it took. The judges stopped the fight. The Holiday Rambler crowd went nuts. Everybody was laughing, even my father.

"In the lilt of Irish laughter
You can hear the angels sing . . ."

Dinner was over and once again he was singing, this time harmonizing with Kerry on a simple tune that everyone knew. Matt and Brendan played their guitars. I plucked my banjo. Clichéd Irish songs aren't usually included in the Leonard family set list, but this one was easy to play, and in the strange RV setting—parked on a small strip of land in a lonely corner of west Texas—it sounded good.

"When Irish eyes are smiling
Sure they steal your heart away . . ."

It also got me to thinking.

Tim, Marge, little Jack, big Jack, and Mike.
Family IQ number doubles with Kevin's arrival
the following year.

My father worked most of his early adult life as a
marketing man for Time, Inc. When I was about
three years old he was transferred to the Chicago office. In 1954, when the company added **Sports Illustrated** to its list of magazines, my dad was one of the
foot soldiers assigned to get it off the ground. He was
well respected and made decent money—enough to
buy a good house in the northern suburb of Glencoe.
The smattering of small, affordable homes that once
made Glencoe and a string of other communities
along the banks of Lake Michigan available to aver-

age families have since been torn down and replaced by bigger, more expensive residences. Anybody buying a house on the north shore now needs a major bankroll.

After moving to Scottsdale, Arizona, in 1968, my dad became involved in the real-estate business. He flourished until the early 1970s, when the Jack Leonards of the world suddenly discovered that a group of Arab oil sheiks could turn millions of lives upside down by turning off a few petroleum spigots. Oil prices shot through the roof, the U.S. economy sank through the floor, and bewildered everyday souls like my father were left stuck in the middle, wondering how their entire life savings could vanish so quickly.

It was a struggle but he bounced back, regaining his financial footing this time in the San Diego area. Wealthy Chicago friends commissioned him to find tracts of land to purchase as short-term investment property. As part of the deal, Dad would also invest in the project, although unlike his rich friends, he had to mortgage his house and everything else to come up with the payment. The original plan was to turn the property over quickly, but when the recession hit in the mid-1980s and real-estate prices dropped, Dad's partners voted to hold on to the land until the economic climate improved. They could use the paper losses as tax write-offs. He didn't have that option. When the mortgage payments came due and the bank threatened foreclosure my brothers and I pooled our resources to keep my parents afloat, a humiliating experience for the proud provider now too old for another chance at redemption.

"Boy, this is what life is all about."

The singing was over and my smiling father was leaning back in his chair.

"And you know," he continued, "I was thinking last night how lucky I am. Lucky to have the family I have, lucky to have the wife I have . . . lucky. Kid from Paterson, New Jersey. I had more luck than I should have had."

"Did you ever imagine that you'd be riding across the country in an RV?" asked Kerry.

"No," he answered emphatically, "especially one driven by your father. I mean, look where we are, in a campsite! Your dad quit Boy Scouts when they told him he had to sleep in a tent . . . for one night."

"That wasn't the reason," I protested. "We weren't in long enough to go camping. Jack and I were kicked out after the first meeting. Jack wouldn't wear the shorts and both of us thought the scarves were way too girlie. Plus, I hadn't gotten over the Cub Scout thing."

"What Cub Scout thing?" asked Brendan.

"The Cub Scout Jamboree," I said. "It was this big showcase held in the New Trier High School gym and our pack was scheduled to do some kind of Indian dance. I missed the meeting where they gave out the feathered headbands and the little leather flaps, so the den mother brought my outfit to the gym that morning and told me to change in the boy's locker room. She never mentioned a thing about underpants."

"Underpants?" laughed Kerry. "This is going to be good."

"I'd watched tons of westerns," I continued, "and never saw any Indians wearing tighty whities under their flaps. Even Tonto, who was a long-pants kind of guy, didn't wear underwear. You could tell because, he didn't have . . ."

"VPL?" asked Margarita. "Visible panty line?"

"Eeew . . . don't say that," groaned Kerry. "I hate that word."

"Panty?" teased Brendan, just to get her goat.

"Anyway," I continued. "The other Cub Scouts showed up wearing the flaps under their regular pants, and when it came time to 'drop trow' right before the dance I got a sick feeling. Nobody else was into authenticity. They were all wearing underwear beneath the flaps. The dance platform was about three feet high and it was ringed with parents, grandparents, kids, and other scouts. I had a rubber spear in one hand and a plastic tomahawk in the other. When the drums started pounding, we started hopping—around and around in a circle. Every time I hopped up, my flap flipped up. Every time my flap flipped up, the laughter level shot up. Because I was holding the spear and the tomahawk, I couldn't use my hands to keep the flaps from flapping, so I tried using my elbow. That just forced me to bend farther down, which made my back flap fly farther up. The crowd went crazy. It still bothers me. I blame scouting."

"Jeez," laughed my father, "we'd never cut it as Indians. Imagine having to start a fire with a couple of sticks? I had enough trouble with the barbecue. Then you'd put about half a can of lighter fluid on it, Mike, and we'd have a mushroom cloud in the backyard."

"I hate the word 'brassiere.' "

All heads turned toward Mom, who flashed an odd smile before continuing her statement.

"But remember how we funny it was when that burger place opened, Brassiere Burgers?"

"You mean Brazier Burgers?" replied Matt.

"Oh, that's how you say it?" Mom asked with a straight face. It was a ruse. She knew how the name was pronounced. The first part of the story, however, was true. A Brazier Burgers sign always did make us scream with laughter.

"Hunting for dinner would be another big problem," I said, returning to the ludicrous notion of our imagined life as Indians.

"I don't know," said Matt. "You stuck it to that mouse pretty good."

"Shit. What mouse?" groaned my mother, lifting her feet off the RV floor.

"There's no mice in the RV," I reassured her. "We're talking about a mouse that was in our basement about fifteen years ago. Remember when Cathy and I went to Ireland and you came to watch the kids?"

Mom responded with a troubled nod.

"Well, I was down in the basement lifting weights on the day we were scheduled to leave and saw a mouse sitting on a shelf. Setting a trap was out of the question, because you'd find it, then freak out. I had to hunt it down on the spot. That's when I thought of the blowgun."

"Why the hell would you have blowgun?" Mom asked.

"Oh, I had done a **Today** story about a guy who made and sold blowguns, as well as the needle-dart ammunition they used," I replied. "He gave me one along with a supply of darts."

"That thing was awesome," said Matt. "Remember Mr. Clean?"

"Mr. Clean?" wondered Margarita.

"Oh, that was from some other story," I explained. "It was a life-size cardboard cutout of Mr. Clean. We used it for blowgun target practice. It became a family activity. I used to wonder what our garbagemen thought after we put it out with the trash. Mr. Clean had about fifteen needle holes around his nose and six thousand or so in his groin area.

"So, I went up to my office on the second floor," I continued. "Got the blowgun and the only two needle darts that could be found and tiptoed back down the basement stairs. The mouse was still sitting on the shelf. I got down in a crouch about twenty feet away, put a dart in the blowgun, and raised it to my mouth. That's when I felt most like an Indian or a jungle native, because I wasn't wearing a shirt and drums were pounding."

"Drums?" asked Margarita.

"Well, sort of," I said. "Our washing machine was screwed up and every now and then a wet ball of corduroy pants or something heavy like that would make it rock back and forth and the sound was kind of drumlike. Anyway, I puffed my cheeks like Dizzy Gillespie and fired the first dart, but it flew an inch over the mouse's head and got stuck in an old paintbrush. The mouse kind of froze and looked at me. What could he have been thinking? I mean, as an upscale suburban mouse he was used to seeing men in suits unless it was casual Friday, and now here's this half-naked guy holding a three-foot-long pipe with a feather hanging from one end. That was his last thought, because I harpooned him with the next shot and down he went. Part of me wanted to bring the dead mouse to a taxidermist and have the head mounted and put over our living-room fireplace, maybe even make a little furry throw rug out of his pelt. What other American can claim to have blow-gunned a mouse? Instead, I swept him into a paper grocery bag and put it in the garbage can."

Young Jack at St. Joseph's Catholic Church in Paterson, New Jersey.

"I'm glad I didn't know about that," my mother groaned. "I would have left. That mouse could have had rabies."

A gust of wind gave the RV a slight shake.

"Maybe it'll rain tonight," I said. "It would be cool to hear rain hitting the RV roof."

Dad peered out the side window and smiled.

"When I was a kid," he began, "my parents took me and my sister to a small bungalow on Mooseback Lake in New Jersey. My mother used to pray for rain at night so she could hear it hit the roof. In Ireland she lived in a house with a thatched roof. There wasn't any sound when the rain hit it. You know, there's no snakes in Ireland. St. Patrick drove them out."

"Well, that's the fable," I said, certain that he would agree. He didn't.

"That's what some scientist is trying to say now. I think St. Patrick drove them out. I never saw a snake."

"We'll get into that some other time," I replied while standing up. "It's late. I have to call home and then I'm going to bed."

With that, my parents said their good nights and went back to their room. The younger folks headed to the Winnebago parked in the adjacent slot. I pulled the bed frame out of the sofa, plugged in the electric pump, filled the mattress with air, then grabbed pillows, sheets and a blanket from a storage cabinet. After making the bed I sat down and called Cathy on my cell phone. We missed each other. Besides having a terrific sense of humor, Cathy is a wonderful person with a forgiving soul, a quality demonstrated far too often thanks to my long history of screw-ups. Through it all, she has been a rock, always standing behind me even while I was cowering **behind** her as she tried to ignite the pilot light on our water heater. Home-maintenance endeavors aren't my strong suit, especially those projects that require thought. Want me to find a new place in the yard for that heavy flowerpot? No problem. Want me to open that biscuit can with a spoon handle? I'd be angry if you didn't ask. Want me to locate the water shutoff valve? The air-conditioning filter? The gas meter? Forget it. Do we even have a gas meter?

I don't do finances either, having zero knowledge of taxes, insurance, stocks, retirement plans, or inter-

Cathy.

est rates. What does rate my interest? Child-rearing. That's my game—from diapers, to feeding, to bedtime stories and beyond. Not that Cathy isn't a great mother—she is—but something about my upbringing, something about my struggles, gave me a perspective on what to do or say when a child needed a lift, or a laugh, or a lecture. My goal was to help my children find their niche, however different that niche might be. And to have fun along the way.

Cathy and I talked for a good twenty minutes, and while she was telling me how anxious Megan and Jamie were, and how they couldn't wait to be parents, I turned my head toward the back of the RV. Through the open venetian blinds I could see my father, dressed in his pj's, kneeling with his hands folded at the foot of the bed. He was saying his prayers. Take away the white hair and the old body and he could've been an eight-year-old boy asking God for a special favor.

Five

Was it some kind of rare west Texas bird species? I sat up in my bed and looked around. The early-morning sunlight, slanting in at odd angles from the edges of the curtained windows, gave the RV interior a spooky feel. The weird, high-pitched chirping sound added an unsettling dimension to the eerie setting. What could it be?

My utter stupidity regarding the workings of the natural world combined with my abject fear of any living thing that doesn't shop for its food created a mental image of a creature bearing horns, fangs, claws, and some kind of venom-spitting mechanism. Whatever it was, one thing was certain: It wasn't normal. Thank God I was safely inside the RV.

Shit.

So was the creature. The noise was coming from my parents' bedroom. The only weapon available was a camera tripod. I grabbed it and slowly approached the door to their room.

"Are you okay?" I shouted.

The chirping stopped for a few seconds. Then . . . in a gasping, choking voice, my mother cried out, "Look at your father's hair!"

I opened the door to their room. My father, still in his pj's, was sitting on the end of the bed, his white hair sticking straight up . . . but mashed together in the middle like a Mohawk. He looked at me sheepishly and said, "I must have slept funny."

Well, funny at least to my mother. His explanation touched off another round of her high-pitched laughing—now positively ID'd as the mystery chirp. She was under the covers, lying on her side, tears rolling down her cheeks.

"He looks like a rooster," I commented in a matter-of-fact voice.

My mother's chirping laugh soared to a higher level. Now she was pounding the pillow. What's with these two? Sixty-plus years of marriage and a bedhead is still funny? Wet-the-bed funny? I walked back into the main area of the RV and started deflating the sofa-bed mattress. Our goal for the day was to get to San Antonio in time to park the RVs at a campsite, then take cabs into the city for a tour of the Alamo and a celebratory dinner for Brendan. It was February sixth, his twentieth birthday.

At six foot four, with curly dark hair and soulful brown eyes, Brendan is a slender, laid-back, funny presence. He's creative, athletic, friendly, and gentle . . . too gentle to excel beyond high school–level baseball, football, and recreational league hockey—the sports that he played. Like all of our kids, Brendan learned to use the video-editing equipment that was set up in my office at home. As high school sophomores, he and his friends created a half-hour cable-access TV program that became a cult hit in our tiny town. The show continued through his high school years and was seen by Marguerite Quinn, a Winnetka resident who sent a tape of the show to her friend Linda Mancuso, an executive at ABC Family. Linda signed Brendan to a deal, and the following summer my nineteen-year-old son was the star and executive producer of his own national show. It was a silly mix of random humor acted out by Brendan and his friends. Our whole family was involved in the production, which was shot on home-movie cameras using our house and neighborhood as a backdrop.

There's never been a TV show like it—real kids in a real house doing what they really do to pass the time on a summer day. We knew it wouldn't be a ratings hit because it didn't have the required amount of adolescent angst. These were just normal teenagers who weren't afraid to act out their everyday, goofy thoughts no matter how "uncool" it might look. That, in itself, was cool. We hoped others would agree.

Cast of **The Brendan Leonard Show:** (left to right) Kevin Sheehan, Kevin Carlson, Ryan Turner, Brendan, Paul Detjen, Michael Carney, Patrick Mohr, and Robbie Karver.

Linda Mancuso backed the unconventional premise by giving my teenage son total creative control, something unheard of in the ultra-restrained television universe. No executive could step in and change the direction of the program. This was a courageous act. Television is all about ratings. Linda, however, was about something else. She was dying of cancer, and this experiment in TV honesty was her last chance to make a statement.

The Brendan Leonard Show debuted on Memorial Day. There was universal praise from the TV critics, but we had no idea how the simple message of the simple show would go over with the public. Would they get it? Would they care? Then, in late June, we got the answer. I was doing some editing work on the second floor of our house when Cathy's voice called up to me.

"Hey Mick, check out the front yard."

I walked into the upstairs family room and pulled the cord on the window shade. A station wagon was parked in front of our house. On our lawn stood a middle-aged couple. They were smiling. A few feet away, three girls hopped up and down in nervous excitement as Brendan and his friends walked from the front steps to talk to them. I went outside and introduced myself to the couple. They told me that their children were obsessed with the program about regular kids in a regular house just being their regular selves. They wanted to see for themselves if it was all as real as it looked. So they drove . . . from Oklahoma.

After an hour's visit they climbed back into their car and headed off to see the rest of the country. As the station wagon drove away we heard screams of delight. A few days later another family arrived. Then another. And another. Through the summer and into the fall—even after **The Brendan Leonard Show** had finished its unique run—people showed up at our front door unannounced. They came from all over the United States and Canada, all relating how the show made them feel better and more confident about their own lives. The visitors were just normal people, not stalker types, and on the days when Brendan wasn't around Cathy and I never felt bothered giving them a tour of our house and the surrounding area. It seemed like the right thing to do.

According to the ratings, **The Brendan Leonard Show** was a bust, a forty-episode counter-programming adventure that failed to attract the kind of numbers needed to justify a second season. But we were certain—and Linda was certain—that it had not been a failure at all. The feedback had been too passionate, the letters of appreciation too heart-felt. A chord had most definitely been struck.

Linda Mancuso died later that year. She was only forty-four and had no children. Her obituary mentioned all the famous programs that she had helped develop, many still airing in syndication. At Linda's memorial service, though, her nurse told Cathy that it was Brendan's videos that Linda wanted to watch in her final days. They made her smile and laugh, even then.

I hope they also made her proud. In back-and-forth e-mails written until the very end, I told Linda about the streams of visitors still traveling to our home. I highlighted many of the emotional quotes from over 200,000 Internet postings that praised the show for finally allowing kids to be kids. Most important, I made a point of letting her know just how grateful we were as a family and promised her that my son would always stay grounded. Linda knew how the TV spotlight could warp a teenager's perspective. But not Brendan's. We would make sure of that.

"Why do I have to do this?" Brendan asked.

My famous son was holding on to the middle of a long, four-inch-wide flexible plastic tube. One end was attached to a spigot on the side of the Holiday Rambler; the other was pushed into a concrete hole in the ground. The time had come to dump the toilet tanks. I had been having nightmarish thoughts of starting the process, then watching in horror as the hose wiggled free from the hole, its business end coming face-to-face . . . with my face. To avoid that kind of life-altering mishap, we put Brendan in charge of holding the hose in place, knowing that at one point something horribly lumpy would be passing by his hands. I almost gagged just writing that line. Brendan did gag feeling the lumpy stuff flow by. Everybody else ran screaming from the scene, further weakening the Leonards' chances of ever acquiring a Roto-Rooter distributorship.

We managed to dump both tanks without any spillage. The psychic splattering was significant, however, and all was quiet as we rolled out the front gate, barely paying any heed to the fiberglass cowboy and the sign that read, "Thanks—Y'all come back." Within minutes we were on Highway 10, heading east toward San Antonio, a little over three hundred miles away. In this wide-open, sparsely populated land, the traffic was light. With Matt driving, I left the front passenger seat to check on my parents in the back.

"I'm feeling a little better today," Mom said in a relaxed voice. "I like it when the highway is flat."

Dad swiveled his easy chair in her direction.

"What's the difference, Marge? We all got to go someday. If we crashed into a truck it would be quick."

Mom's face darkened. "Jesus, Jack, don't say that! I want to go in my sleep."

My father leaned back in the chair, folding his hands across his lap. "I'm gonna take it as it comes," he said. "I have no control of it and no fear of it."

"Of death?" I asked. "Why not?"

"Well, I believe there's a hereafter," he replied, "and a heaven. I think if you've earned it, you'll make it, and if you haven't, you won't."

"I'm not good with heights," Mom muttered to herself while looking out the window.

"I think it's some kind of eternal peace," Dad continued. "I think we'll see our friends and our loved ones. I want to see my mother and father. I want to see my younger sister and my brother . . . maybe run into Tommy Dorsey and he can play a few tunes for us."

"I think we'll be feathers," Mom said.

"Huh?" I turned to face my mother. She was still staring out the window, head tilted upward, squinted eyes focused on a great, white billowy cloud floating by.

"There's too many people in the world and they're too heavy, especially nowadays," she explained. "I think we'll all be feathers."

"Made out of feathers? I asked. "Or would each person be one feather?"

"Just one feather," she answered with a serious look. "That's the only way we'd all fit. I think most of us will go."

"It's big, Marge, big." My father's hands were now folded behind his head, and he too was staring out the window and up at the clouds. "We'll fit."

"But I wonder about something," my mother added. "I have friends whose husbands have died and they remarried, some of them two or three times. You're supposed to see your loved ones up there, so who would you be with . . . one, two, or three? Or all three at the same time? I don't know."

There was a pause, and then my mother frowned and turned her head toward my dad, then to me, saying, "If I see your father up there and he's hanging around with someone else, he'll be in trouble. That's if he goes first. One thing for sure, he'll be talking to somebody."

Dad didn't hear her.

"But you'll probably live till you're ninety-eight," she added, turning now to face my father. "I'll go toes-up first and you'll be movin' in with some Asian."

"Asian?" I asked in a surprised tone.

"Oh, he loves Asians," Mom explained. "He's crazy about black hair. My mother had black hair and when it turned, it was shiny, like silver. It was beautiful. That's what happens when people have black, black hair. It doesn't turn gray, it turns silver. If I didn't color mine it would look like wheat."

"Marge," Dad chimed in, "you had the most beautiful hair in all of Paterson. Long ringlets. Reddish brown. Beautiful."

"But now look at it," she grumbled, pressing down on a wayward wave above her ear. "The lady who colored it last really goofed up. It's too dark. I look like a cheap hooker. I may stop coloring it soon because it's getting to be a pain. Why doesn't that Dick Clark guy hang it up?"

"Why?" I asked sarcastically. "Does he dye his hair?"

"No," laughed my father. "Hey, remember the head of hair on Bob Richards, the Wheaties guy when you were growing up, Mike?"

"Oh yeah, the Reverend Bob," I nodded, recalling a ten-year span of time when his smiling face was on every Wheaties box in the land.

Mom fished for something at the bottom of her big purse. She didn't appear to be paying attention but then said, "How the hell could he pull a boat with his teeth?"

My father looked confused. "What boat?"

"I think she means Jack LaLanne," I said. "I'm pretty sure he's still alive, and . . ."

"Marge, you know, Bob Richards," interrupted my father, "he was the Olympic pole-vault champion in the fifty-six Olympics. Remember we brought him out to North Shore Country Club to play golf for that **Sports Illustrated** promotion? His foursome was about to tee off and they couldn't find him. Then his shoes hit the ground. He was way up in a tree and didn't want to come down. The other guys in the group, real corporate types, just looked at each other. They didn't know what to say. Richards was an eccentric guy, but fun to be around. That one Olympic medal carried him the rest of his life. Speeches. Commercials. Wheaties boxes."

"That doesn't happen anymore," I said. "Heroes don't last. You win a gold medal now and everybody knows your name until the minute the Olympics are over, then you're old news. Chew 'em up and spit 'em out. In today's world, Richards's fame wouldn't last a week. And it wouldn't come for just winning the pole vault. That's not enough. He'd need some kind of sad story line, like his mother dying two weeks before the Olympics. Her ashes would've been dumped into his pole, and every time he planted it for a jump there'd be a little poof and a small cloud of his mom would shoot out the top. And they'd keep showing it from different angles in super-slow motion, maybe even with a picture of his mother superimposed in the background."

My mother nodded in deep thought, then looked at my father and said, "How the hell can a man pull a boat with his teeth?"

It was about noon when we got off the highway to buy gas in a tiny Texas town in the middle of nowhere. My dad stepped out of the RV and walked to the little gas station–convenience store. I followed him in, noticing that he was now wearing cowboy boots and his left pant leg was inadvertently stuck into the top of one of the boots. Inside the store, an older woman stood at the register and Dad smiled at her as he put a newspaper on the counter and fished for coins in his pocket.

"Boy, I tell you, this is one big state," he exclaimed in his usual cheerful manner.

"Is it a big state?" she replied in an oddly quizzical way.

My dad paused for a second or two. "I'm sorry," he said quickly. "I forgot that I have to buy a few more things."

He turned to his left and started pulling postcards off a small swiveling rack. Then he hustled over to a dusty section of shelves, grabbing a box of Kleenex, a roll of paper towels, a few pens, a map, and some tape. Back at the counter, he scooped up a bunch of candy bars. I knew the drill. He was trying to be nice. The way she'd reacted to his greeting struck him a certain way, and now he was putting the coins back into his pocket and taking out a clip of bills. My dad gave the elderly woman a twenty, told her to keep the change, and then reached out to shake her hand.

"Thank you very much," he said with a big smile. "You're a nice lady."

As I watched my father carry a bag of unwanted items back toward the RV, his pant leg still stuck in his boot, I found myself wondering how he made it through life. He's too generous, too sensitive, an easy mark. There are hundreds of stories to support that supposition. Here are two.

Michelangelo in a Paper Hat

I came home from high school one afternoon and was startled by the sight of a large African-American man standing in our kitchen. He wore a paper bag on his head. It was a big brown grocery bag with a panel ripped out for his face to show. The ripped section was rolled up to form a coiled visor above his eyes. He had a paint roller in his hand and a grin on his face. The only sound came from a steady pitter-patter of liquid hitting paper. Looking up, I saw great gobs of white paint swirled across the ceiling. Drips cascaded onto the top of the bag, the floor, the counter, the stove, the toaster, everywhere.

"Hey there little man, I'm Robert."

"Hi, I'm Mike."

"Glad to meet you, Mike. Your daddy hired me to paint the kitchen. I met him at Chicago Stadium last week. I was parking cars. He's a good man."

He sure is, but he pays for that reputation— often twice, as he did in this situation, paying Robert, then paying the professional crew to right all of Robert's many artistic wrongs.

When Irish Leaves Are Burning

To this day we don't know how the small stranger with an Irish accent ended up raking leaves in our backyard. This was at a juncture in our nation's history when leaf burning was allowed. My youngest brother, Kevin, only a first-grader at the time but already a Rhodes scholar in the study of screwball behavior, had pulled up a lawn chair to analyze the stranger's odd movements. In his landmark study, Kevin noted three major deviations from the standard suburban leaf-raking technique:

1) Frequent gulps from a small silver flask seemed to affect the raker's balance.
2) The leaves were piled against the wall of our wooden garage.
3) Gasoline was used as an accelerant.

The man with the funny accent disappeared soon after the flames began crawling up the side of the garage. In a footnote to his study, Kevin surmised that the giant fireball had inspired some sort of religious awakening in the fellow, judging from his weepy cries of "Oh, Jaysus" and "Sweet mother of God" before running off.

The little man never came by the house again, but we're certain that my father had given him a generous up-front payment. And why not? The Irishman had provided Kevin with the thrill of a lifetime by arranging for real, live firemen to race through our yard with hoses and axes. By the time they left, waving to a smiling Kevin from the back of their truck, our garage and everything in it had been reduced to a smoldering black heap.

"Why is Davy Crockett the most famous person who died at the Alamo?"

Brendan posed that question from the front seat of a crowded van-type taxi heading for downtown San Antonio.

"I don't know," I answered. "Because he had a TV show?"

It was about three-thirty in the afternoon. We had parked the RVs in a campsite on the outskirts of the city and were now heading in to see the Alamo, Brendan continuing with the kind of basic questioning that our family loves to exploit.

"I mean, I don't hear as much about Colonel Travis as I do about Davy Crockett."

"Davy had a cooler hat," Matt replied in a deadpan manner before singing the famous "Davy Crockett" melody with new lyrics: "Colonel . . . Colonel Travis . . ."

"Why isn't it pronounced **coll-on-el**?" called out Kerry from the backseat. "There's no 'R' in colonel, so why do they say **ker-nal**?"

"Don't get me started," I said. "Why do people use the term 'pro bono'? Why don't they just say 'for free'? It's the same amount of letters and it's in English."

"Or 'quid pro quo'?" Margarita asked. "That's Latin for 'tit for tat.' "

"That one really stumps me," I replied. "It means 'an equal exchange,' but if you actually asked people what they'd rather have, a tit or a tat, who would want a tat? Everybody I know would go for the tit. Hands down. No question."

We were all laughing at the silliness of the conversation when the cab dropped us a few blocks from the Alamo. The historic structure is surrounded by regular city buildings and is a surprising sight when first encountered.

"No wonder they got their asses kicked," said Brendan. "It's tiny."

"It sure is," Mom agreed, "but I just love places like this. I never thought that I'd ever see it."

A smattering of tourists mingled in front of the Alamo. Before going inside, I asked my parents to pose for a picture by the famous facade. Just as I was framing the scene, Dad disappeared from the viewfinder and started to sing:

"Across the alley from the . . . Alamo
Lived a pinto pony and a . . . Navajo
Who sang a sort of Indian 'Hi-de-ho'
To the people passing by."

"What kind of song is that?" I asked, looking around to see if any of the bystanders had heard him singing.

"Oh, that was a big hit about the time you were born," he gushed while moving back into the camera frame. "The Mills Brothers sang it. They were great. **'Oh . . .'** " Suddenly he was gone again.

". . . The pinto spent his time a-swishing
   flies
And the Navajo watched the lazy skies
And very rarely did they ever rest their eyes
On the people passin' by . . ."

"All right, enough of that song," I pleaded. "Let's get this picture taken before they close the place."

Dad shuffled into the frame, but before I could get him to look at me and smile he turned to my mother and started talking.

"That was a great song, wasn't it Marge? Why aren't there any singers like the Mills Brothers anymore?"

"Because they're old news, Jack. Get with the program. It's P. Diddy now."

My father's expression turned sour.

"Why the hell . . . ?"

Click.

I couldn't wait any longer. The picture was taken and we went inside. Historic places like the Alamo always fascinate me, especially the collections of personal items and individual stories. Unfortunately, my search for those treasured gems was aborted within minutes when I glanced up from a scary collection of 1830s-era amputation saws and noticed that my parents were missing. My mother had scooted off to the gift shop, where I found her buying an Alamo coffee mug with "JACK" stamped on the front. Dad had walked out a side door and was sitting on a bench by the street.

"Well, that was worth it," I said to him with sarcasm.

"Wasn't it great?" he answered enthusiastically.

"But you never even . . ." Before I could express my doubt about the sincerity of his statement, another voice intruded from the rear.

"Look what I got you, Jack." Mom pulled the white coffee mug from the bag and tilted it different ways so he could see all its wonderful facets.

"That's terrific, Marge. Some place, isn't it?"

It wasn't yet 6:00 P.M. when we celebrated Brendan's twentieth birthday at a Mexican restaurant on San Antonio's touristy River Walk. The waiter brought a small cake to the table, and in the dimness of the half-empty restaurant the lighted candles added a soft glow to Brendan's face. He could have been having the time of his life in college had he not taken a semester off to help chaperone two old people on their final journey across America. I stared at him and started feeling it again—that overpowering sensation of time speeding by. How could my baby be twenty? How could my baby Megan be having her own baby in three weeks?

Later that night I stepped outside the RV and called home. Cathy and I talked about the bittersweet aspect of birthday celebrations. We no longer had a teenager in the family. All of our children were now in their twenties and thirties. How had it happened so fast? My wife then recalled a conversation that took place twenty-one years earlier. We were visiting her parents in Florida and one night after dinner, while Matt, Megan, and Kerry were entertaining their grandparents, Cathy and I walked out to a small dock on the waterway behind the house. That's where she told me she wanted to have another baby. I cautioned her about the looming demands of my NBC job. A presidential election and the Olympics would be taking place in 1984. What if I had to cover them? What if I had to be away for weeks at a time? Cathy's answer was about babies, but it could just as easily have been about a whole bunch of other subjects. She said that people never regret following their heart . . . their regrets come from not following it.

Six

"What do you think of Phil Mickelson, Jack?"

Silence.

"JACK!"

"Jeez, Marge, what? I didn't hear you."

"You gotta get those ears checked!" Mom shouted. "I asked what you thought of Phil Mickelson. He seems like a nice guy."

We were rolling along Highway 10 approaching Beaumont, Texas. Despite repeated warnings, Dad had once again parked his butt in a flimsy wooden folding chair at the dinette table, a winning solitaire hand apparently well worth the risk of being hurled through the windshield due to a sudden stop. On the opposite side of the RV, Mom was sitting sideways on the couch, a pile of newspapers in her lap. Something she read must have triggered the question about the golfer.

"Yeah, I do think he's a nice guy," my father replied. "Say, Mike, I read somewhere that a lot of pro golfers are doing what we're doing, traveling the country in RVs, going from event to event."

"I read about that too," I said from the driver's seat. "That's one of those hard jobs that looks easy . . . being a pro golfer."

To my right, Matt nodded his head in agreement. "And what makes it so hard is having to wear those dorky clothes. ON TV!"

"I get bored with golf on TV," my dad interjected. "I only watch the last hole, but if it comes down to the last putt I turn it off because I end up feeling sorry for the loser."

"That's like me with my books," added my mother. "I always read the last page first. I don't like surprises."

"More people would watch golf on TV if they followed my suggestions," I said, plucking my banjo practice belt as I drove. "First put a chain-link fence around the course, a really high one to keep the fans on the outside. Then release one hungry lion on the front nine and another hungry lion on the back nine. Not knowing the whereabouts of the lions would make the golfers hustle to get off the course as quickly as they could, speeding up the play. The element of danger would add drama because everybody's fair game to the lions, not just the leaders. Of course, the TV ratings would go up because you'd attract a lot of new viewers who don't normally watch golf. Imagine channel surfing onto a golf event and hearing the announcer say, 'Ernie Els with a thirty-foot putt for a birdie . . . if he makes this he will be . . . Oh my goodness! Stewart Cink is on the run! Let's go to six, where Cink is being chased down the fairway by . . . is that Simba? Yes, it's Simba. Look at Cink go!'

"I don't think anybody would change channels, do you?"

There was no response from my parents. Dad had resumed his solitaire game and Mom had her head buried in the Rand McNally road atlas.

"I guess they don't think much of my idea," I muttered to Matt.

He nodded. "Yeah, that's okay. They're not the right viewing demographic anyway. I'd watch."

Long journeys down boring highways lend themselves to goofy conversations. So does the experience of being raised in a household that saw humor in almost any situation. I was lucky. My childhood family package had it all: four boys, a nutty mother, a jovial dad, a live-in grandmother who never ratted us out, a small-town neighborhood teeming with kids our age, and at the end of the street three square blocks of stores, diners, soda fountains, gas stations, back alleys, fire escapes, a movie theater, and a gazillion places for kids like us to run and hide. On top of all

Three of four Leonard boys in their Sunday worst.

that, right between our block and the village was a park . . . a park with a crab apple tree! All mischievous boys are created with two primal yearnings: one is to climb something, and the other is to throw something. God is good. In the middle of our little Eden he gave us something to climb, filled with a never-ending supply of something to throw. What is more perfect to throw than a crab apple? Nothing, unless you're inside a movie theater, and that is why the Creator also gave us Dots.

The Glencoe movie theater was three blocks from our house. My mother would give my brothers and me fifty cents each and off we'd go. Back then fifty cents would cover admission, candy or popcorn, and a soda. Most of us chose Dots because of the candy's unparalleled versatility. The fruit-flavored gumdrops were good to eat but even better to throw—either right out of the box or after being sucked on for a minute to soften them up and make them stick to the screen or the wall. Milk Duds could also be eaten and thrown, but they weren't as chewy as Dots and were therefore a little more difficult to grip and rip. Occasionally a handful of Good & Plentys and Jujubes were launched, but only when trying to blanket a section in scattershot.

During Saturday matinees the theater would be jammed with kids and the air filled with candied missiles. It must have been a nightmare for the teenage ushers in their ill-fitting red tuxedo jackets. Called on to quell a disturbance in a front-row section, the usher's silhouetted figure—moving across the bright screen—might as well have been the outline of a tin duck sliding back and forth in a shooting gallery. The poor ushers also served as janitors, cleaning up the mess when the theater emptied out. Sometimes we helped with the mopping in a roundabout way. When movies were boring, my brothers and I held races. Starting in the back row, we spread out, gave a hand signal, and then took off toward the front row. Running wasn't allowed. We had to slither—on our stomachs—under the seats. Spilled Coke, flattened pieces of Charleston Chews, fractured shards of Necco Wafers, half-eaten Sno Caps, dropped Jawbreakers, spit-out Chiclets, discarded Cinnamon Tooth Picks, fragments of Oh Henry! bars—all of that and more was glued to our clothes when we popped up a few feet from the screen.

Good movies occasionally commanded the respect of the audience. Nothing would be thrown. Ushers would be spared. When **Earth vs the Flying Saucers** came to the Glencoe Theater we stared at the screen in bug-eyed silence. You could have heard a Raisinet drop. Predicting crowd behavior, however, is an imperfect science. That's why management was caught off guard when the powder keg blew during an early showing of **The Seventh Voyage of Sinbad**. We considered it one of the greatest films of all time and might have excused the mistake had it centered on the giant two-headed bird or some other minor character, but no, this involved the Cyclops. In the early scenes he had one horn on the top of his head. Later on in the movie he suddenly had . . . **two horns**! Sinbad didn't seem to notice, but we sure did and peppered the screen in protest.

Hell hath no fury, though, like a Leonard boy scorned, and our butts were scorned good on that fateful Saturday afternoon in 1958. Jack, Timmy, and I got to the theater early, lured by two powerful words written on the previous week's coming attractions poster in the glass window adjacent to the ticket booth: **Damn Yankees.** We couldn't believe our eyes. A movie about baseball and swearing! This would be our finest hour. Or so we thought.

I won't go into the details about the riot. Let's just say that there was a thirty-second period of shocked silence when the singing started. Jack looked at me. I looked at Timmy. Our jaws dropped. Our eyes widened. **Damn Yankees** was a damn musical . . . with no swearing! That's when the first Dot ricocheted off Tab Hunter's cheek. In the blink of an eye, Gwen Verdon took a Milk Dud in the eye. Then the skies opened up, raining Atomic Fire Balls, bubblegum cigars, wax bottles, wax lips, Root Beer Barrels, Chunkys, Zagnuts, Pez (and dispensers), Slo Pokes, and Bit O' Honeys launched from every corner of the theater. The other candy throwers might not have shared our feelings of betrayal, but they sure did share our sense of fun. And this was the definition of fun: ducking and running through the rows of seats, aiming at each other instead of the now forgotten movie, our screams and laughs drowning out that horrible singing.

It was a different time. Lots of small towns had their own movie theaters and kids would walk or ride their bikes to the shows, streaming in from all directions without a parent in sight. Most summer days, in fact, were spent without a parent in sight. They assumed that we would figure out how to pass the time. And we did, assuming what they didn't know wouldn't hurt them. And they didn't know. And it

Mike and Jack practice a "Joy Buzzer" handclasp.

didn't hurt them. It hurt us. But we lived and we learned.

My best friend, Ricky Leslie, for instance, learned never to ride a bike at full speed through a freshly painted wooden tunnel. Actually it wasn't really a tunnel; it was a wooden drive-through structure at the entrance to the Glencoe Women's Club. The painters had attached a "wet paint" sign to the middle of a copper wire strung tightly across the drive-through entrance. Some fool (perhaps one of us) removed the sign but left the copper wire in place. Ricky never saw it as he pedaled toward the tunnel at Mach 1. The bike kept going. Ricky didn't, catching the wire right below his Adam's apple. Later conversations with our friend Buddy, who was riding with Ricky but ducked, gave us the impression that the incident unfolded in a rather beautiful manner because never before had real life so closely resembled a **Road Runner** cartoon.

Ricky's injury was big news on our block. But the bigger news involved his parents. They lodged a complaint. That was unheard of. Ricky's neck was sliced from ear to ear. He could have been killed. The authorities agreed, and before long a sizable settlement check was issued. The amount was stunning. Two hundred dollars, to cover medical bills.

Our mishaps weren't as cinematic as Ricky's, just more frequent. We fell off garage roofs and tumbled out of bunk beds, caught our toes in spokes and our fingers in car doors, took baseballs to the head and

ice balls to the face. It was all part of growing up—
the stitches, the splints, the black eyes, and the
bloody noses. Family photographs from that era
often show one of the Leonard boys in some kind of
bandaged state. I don't have the stats to prove it, but
the frequency of injuries per household seemed to
climb in relation to the number of boys per household. So did the frequency of bizarre phone calls to
the family doctor:

> **"Hi, Dr. Eisenberg. This is Marge Leonard.
> Sorry to bother you again but I found our pet
> turtle in Kevin's mouth. I don't know how
> long it was in there. Will he get salmonella?"**

> **"Hi, Dr. Eisenberg, Marge Leonard again.
> About three or four days ago Timmy shoved
> a colored glass Christmas ornament up his
> nose. It's about the size of a cat's-eye marble.
> We don't know how to get the thing out and
> he has class pictures coming up."**

That's the kind of stuff that happened in a house
with four boys. Our sense of play, our sense of humor,
our sense of life, our lack of sense . . . everything was
shaped by that dynamic. Through the years I've often
wondered how our lives would have changed if a girl
had been part of that mix. There's no doubt that I'd be
a different person today had my sister lived.

Her name was Ann. She was born in 1944, two

The Leonard quadruplets on
Christmas morning. A seedling
from our aluminum tree was
planted but never grew.

years before Jack, but then she died. That's all I really
know. My parents do not talk about Ann. We
stopped asking a long time ago.

"Well, do I look like a phony or do I look like a Texas
Ranger?" Dad tugged the front of a big brown cowboy hat, tilting it lower on his head. We were in a
western-wear clothing store in east Texas.

"You look like old Jim Shoulders," the man behind the counter answered.

"You sure know how to make a sale," laughed my father. "How can I not buy the hat after you tell me that I look like the greatest rodeo cowboy who ever lived? Was he from Texas?"

"No," the man said. "Shoulders is from Henryetta, Oklahoma."

"What great names!" my father gushed. "Jim Shoulders. Henryetta, Oklahoma. It just fits."

"Yeah," I said. "I love the names of those rodeo guys. I covered the national finals once and remember looking at the list of bull-riding champions. Kid Fletcher. Freckles Brown. Lane Frost. Tuf Hedeman. And the town names where some of the other guys came from: Mesquite, Texas . . . Red Lodge, Montana . . . Hugo, Oklahoma . . . Sombrero Butte, Arizona . . . lot of guys from Henryetta."

The man behind the counter had taken the cowboy hat from my dad and placed it on a weird steaming contraption to stretch it out a bit. "And what's your name, sir?" my father asked.

"Well . . ." the man drawled. "How's this for a conversation starter? My name is Bond . . . James Bond."

"Wow, you sound just like him," I joked, getting a laugh out of James and everybody else. "This must be a hot spot for problem names. A long time ago I did a story on a guy in east Texas named Joe Blow. I found him through directory assistance . . . Mr. and Mrs. Joe Blow and the four Blow boys. Nice family. When I first called him on the phone, I explained who I was and told him that I wanted to come down to his town with a camera crew and do a **Today** show piece on what it's like to go through life with a name like Joe Blow. He tried to beg off, saying, 'Aw you don't want to hang around with me, I'm just an ordinary guy.' I went, 'Yeah, I know. You're Joe Blow!' Well, we flew down and spent a few days with Mr. and Mrs. Joe Blow and the four Blow boys, and the whole time we were there Joe kept saying, 'I really don't know why you find this interesting.' Then right as we were packing up to leave, a light bulb must have gone off in his head, because he looked at me and said, 'Hey Mike, I don't know if you'd be interested in this or not but I have an old yellowed newspaper article with a picture of me meeting a guy named John Doe.' "

James Bond laughed at the story and nodded his head. "Yeah, I've heard all the jokes. I wish I had double-o-seven's money. I wouldn't be shapin' hats."

With that, his wife walked over from the front counter. It was a nice store, full of jeans, shirts, boots, belts, and hats, all neatly arranged under framed and autographed photos of past and present rodeo champions. James Bond finished steaming my father's hat and then made sure that we knew he was joking about his wish for another way of life.

Hop-a-long Jack at the Bar B Western
Store in Vidor, Texas.

·"I'm real thankful," he told us while standing with
his wife. "I've had this store for about twenty-seven
years. The Lord's been good to us. We've done all
right."

"You sure have," agreed Dad, who then circled
back through the store grabbing shirts, belt buckles,
cowboy-style handkerchiefs, and whatever else he
could carry to the register.

Later that day we parked the RVs at the Boomtown
USA RV and Fishing Park near Beaumont, Texas. It
was a little sliver of land with a highway on one side
and a small lake on the other. We could see the tops

of a few stores on the other side of the road, and Brendan offered to hike through the concrete tunnel to scout the area for take-out food. His suggestion jostled the Worry Giant out of his brief slumber inside my mother's head. The Worry Giant had been hospitalized for exhaustion after the stressful early stages of the journey. Doctors had prescribed a week of bed rest, but my mother needed to know that everything wasn't all right, so she opened the blinds and gave him a good shake and now he was up and ornery.

"I don't think Brendan should go over there," my mother whined. "The world is full of creeps."

"Brendan's twenty years old." I said. "He'll be fine. The stores are only about three hundred yards from here."

"But we don't know who lives here," Mom persisted. "There might be gangbangers."

Brendan was nearly out the door when I stopped him. The conversation had reminded me of a story that my father told a long time ago. It was about his first trip to Ireland. He went by himself. He was twelve years old. I thought Brendan and everybody else should hear the story, just to get a better idea of how life has changed in the span of two generations, so I asked my father to tell it.

"You had to go by boat," Dad began. "Lindbergh had just flown across the ocean in a little plane, but that was like going to the moon back then. There wasn't any passenger service, not that distance. There were blimps that made the trip, but only rich people could do that."

As my father continued talking, I noticed that it was happening again. I was listening closer. I was paying more attention to the details of his story. It was odd. I knew my parents as well as any child could, but something was prompting me to look deeper, something was pushing me to learn more, something was telling me that I would soon be seeing my father, my mother, and myself in a whole new light.

"I don't know why they sent me," Dad continued. "Maybe one less mouth to feed, it was the Depression . . . maybe to protect me from getting sick after Tommy and Anna died.

"I was one of four children. My older sister, Mary, and I lived through childhood. Tommy and Anna didn't. Diphtheria killed Tommy when he was five. Anna died from scarlet fever when she was two. There were no antibiotics in those days. A child would get sick and before the week was over the rest of the family would be weeping by a headstone. I was six years old when Anna's little white coffin sat on a table in the front room of our house. Five days earlier I was teaching her how to ride a tricycle. She was wearing a pink hat and a pink coat. Her curly hair was dark red. She was laughing. That's what I remember.

"So they packed a little suitcase for me and sewed a string to my hat so it wouldn't blow into the ocean. My mother wrote a list of instructions on a piece of paper. Get off the boat in Queenstown. Take a train to Dublin. Your aunt will meet you at the train station. Make sure it's your aunt. Sometimes bad people trick little children. Don't stand too close to the railing on the boat."

The light streaming through the RV window was falling on my father's face as he continued with the story. He looked old. There was a slight shake to his hand as he reached for a cookie. His eyes were watery. I tried to imagine those same eyes on a twelve-year-old boy as he turned around from the gangplank to bid his parents farewell.

"The ship was named **The Baltic**," Dad went on. "It was a seagoing vessel and I was its youngest passenger. I had a room with another man. He was a Methodist minister. He was in the bottom bunk and I was in the top. It was six days on the ocean before we landed at Queenstown in County Cork. Queenstown is now called Cobh. They changed the name after Ireland broke from England. When we got there the tide was out, so we had to climb into what they call a tender—kind of a big rowboat—to take us to shore. We were about a mile out. It was two in the morning. An old lady sitting next to me kept hollering, 'Where's me trunk? Where's me trunk?' The guy steering the tender finally said, 'You're like a bloody elephant, your trunk is right in front of you.' I thought that was funny.

"When we got to the dock, I picked up my suitcase and started walking toward the town. A man I recognized from the boat asked where I was headed. I told him that I was looking for the train station because I had to meet my aunt in Dublin. He said that there'd be no trains to Dublin at this time of night and asked what I planned to do next. I said that I would probably just stand by the train station and wait. He told me that he had a room at the hotel and said that I could sleep there. And I did. Imagine that today with all the nuts in the world!

"I really must have looked lost wandering around the dock, alone at two in the morning. So I slept in the man's room that night, nothing happened, and I took a train to Dublin the next morning. It arrived in the afternoon, and when I got off it the engines were hissing and steam was blowing. People were rushing everywhere. I stood in the middle of it all and then a woman came up to me and said, 'Are you Jack? I'm your aunt from Cavan. I'm Uncle Benny's wife.' I did what my mom told me to do in her note and asked her how I could be sure that she was my aunt. She pulled out a letter from her bag and I recognized my mother's handwriting, so off I went with her. The two of us got on another train that went to Cavan, about sixty miles west of Dublin. We arrived in Cavan at night and my aunt passed me off to someone else, an uncle named Phil Sheridan, who drove me in an old car to a small farmhouse on the edge of the town. It was the house my mom grew up in, and it was just like she said it would be. Thatched roof. Dirt floor. No toilet. No running water.

"The people were all sitting in the one room in front, smoking and drinking tea. They came to see Annie Smith's boy and they started asking lots of questions about my mother, about my father, about our house, about America. Then somebody said, 'The lad must be tired,' so my aunt took me into a back room and I got my pajamas from the suitcase. I had two sets, a light pair and a heavy pair. My mom's note said to wear the heavy pair in Cavan. It was flannel with a high neck and some kind of Asian design, like a dragon, on the back. I put it on and walked out and everybody started to laugh. One of the men said, 'What the hell are ya gettin' dressed up for just to go to bed?'

"The bed was small, and my seven-year-old cousin was already asleep in it. I got in next to him. A little while later another uncle climbed in. He was about forty and was still wearing his clothes. They smelled like smoke. The men slept in the same clothes they worked in. That's why they laughed at my pajamas."

"Wait a minute," Brendan interrupted, "You bunked with a minister on the boat, then you shared a hotel room with a stranger, and now you're sleeping in the same bed with a forty-year-old uncle and a seven-year-old cousin?"

"That's the way it was," Dad said. "They had no room. And so many bodies in a small place made things warmer. The houses weren't heated; there was just a little fireplace in the main room where they burned the peat. So I ended up in the middle. Slept in that little bed with the both of them the whole time I was there."

"And how long was that?"

"Oh, it was over a year. I worked on the farm. Helped out in the bar. Never went to school. It was great."

"But how much time passed before your parents in New Jersey knew that you'd arrived safely?" I asked, shaking my head at the mere thought of anybody in my world cutting their child loose even for an afternoon.

"Oh jeez," he said, "not until someone got around to writing a letter, then mailing it. Everything went by boat, so I'm guessing my parents didn't know whether I got there or not for about a month, maybe longer."

"So Brendan," I said sarcastically, "I'm going to go out on a limb and let you walk over to those stores. But for God's sakes, take your cell phone and call us every few minutes."

"Shit," Mom muttered in all seriousness. "Gang-bangers kill people for their cell phones."

Seven

"Welcome to Louisiana."

The sign on Highway 10 marked the gateway to another set of adventures, but my mother wasn't in a position to see it. She hadn't yet emerged from the RV bathroom despite my repeated shouts that the bridge was now behind us. I knew she was still alive because a muffled slew of curse words drifted into the main cabin. The narrow bridge had been scary, looming high above the river separating Louisiana from Texas. The giant RV put our lines of sight above the bridge's sidewalls, and at times it felt as if a good wind might topple us into the abyss. Ten minutes after the crossing, my mother finally emerged from the bathroom and settled back into her defensive posture on the couch, hands fused to the armrests, feet screwed to the floor.

Then the shaking started.

Books, magazines, newspapers, plastic water bottles, apples, bananas, cereal boxes—anything that wasn't strapped down began cascading off tables and shelves. We'd been on some bumpy highways, but none like this. It was weird. There were no visible potholes or dips in the pavement, yet it felt as if we were on a small boat plowing our way through choppy seas. Up and down. Up and down.

"They must have had a blind engineer lay this one out!" shouted Dad, holding the top of his cowboy hat.

A Cheerios box skidded off the kitchen counter and onto Mom's lap.

"What kind of state is this?" she whined.

"It's a great state," I replied, trying to sound calm. "I love Louisiana, especially southern Louisiana, Cajun country. I love the town names: Mamou, Opelousas, Maurice. I love the music. The people are characters. So they have a few crappy roads. It's a small price to pay for greatness."

"Greatness, my ass," groaned Mom as the pitching and rolling intensified.

A few long minutes later, the bouncing finally stopped. We had made it out of the Class C asphalt rapids and were now sailing along on a smoother stretch of highway. My mother pried her fingers from the armrest and straightened her white floppy tennis hat—an encouraging sign. Up until this point, her standard response to scary driving situations had been to flip me off. I interpreted her restraint as a possible turning point in our RV relationship.

We traveled east through Lake Charles, Evangeline, Mermentau, Duson, and Lafayette, the odd nature of the swampy Louisiana landscape making me feel more and more excited for what would follow. Up until now we hadn't had much time to mix with the locals, but that would change in bayou country. I picked up my cell phone and called Jennifer Angelle, a young woman who worked at the visitor's center in Breaux Bridge, the town where we were headed. I had been there on a **Today** show story and Jennifer had been a big help, introducing me to some of the area's more colorful personalities. Could they handle a couple more?

**"Should auld acquaintance be forgot
And never brought to mind . . ."**

I had no idea why my father suddenly started singing that song. He was leaning back in the recliner, his cowboy hat tipped up, his eyes half closed. It was late morning. Breaux Bridge was fifteen minutes away and there was a lot to see. He wasn't looking.

**"Should auld acquaintance be forgot
And days of auld lang syne . . ."**

I've heard the song a million times. What the hell does it mean? The melody is sweet, though, and Dad has a good singing voice, so it sounded nice. Then, out of the blue, the damn things snuck up on me again. Tears. I had been fighting them my whole life. They come easily to me, and that's a problem when you're one of four boys. When I was young my brothers would razz me. "Look!" they would shout, "he's got sprinkly eyes again." Physical pain was hardly ever the cause. I could handle broken noses, fat lips, and black eyes. It was the other stuff, the sad moments, that made my eyes water. And to me, this was a sad moment, hearing my dad, my very old dad, sing that song as we rolled through another part of the country that he would never see again. Was he feeling the same emotion?

No.

That became evident when he launched into the next verse . . . with new words:

"It may be so for all we know
But it sounds so very queer,
So tell your jokes to other folks
Don't spread your bullshit here."

Mom wasn't paying any attention to his singing. She was busy writing.

"Sending off another postcard, huh?" Matt asked as he walked past her to get a Coke from the refrigerator. "Who is this one going to?"

"Oh, just a lady who used to live next door to us," she replied while continuing to write. "She's in her nineties, lives in some retirement place in Florida now. I like to write to old people. I think I do it because when my mom was living with us, I'd go out to the mailbox and when I'd come back in she would ask, 'Anything for me?' and I'd always have to say no. That made me feel sad."

For all of her wiseass quirks, my mother has a soft heart. It shows in her writing.

Sometimes it shows too much.

Back in 1980 I was worried about my standing in the broadcast world. I had just been hired by the **Today** show, and the initial lack of feedback concerning my work was troubling. That's why I was so happy when the first piece of mail arrived from the NBC PR Department. It was a copy of the standard network reply letter written to thank people for taking the time to offer their opinions. Also in the envelope was a copy of the viewer's letter. A fan letter! Reading the first line made me lightheaded.

"In case you are unaware of it, you have a young, attractive, intelligent, humorous threat to Andy Rooney."

The note went on to suggest that I be given more airtime. A woman named Francis Sweeney had signed it. I felt humbled that a stranger would actually take the time to honor my efforts. Knowing that the brass at NBC had seen the letter gave me additional encouragement, because it proved to them that the audience appreciated the offbeat quality of my work.

A short time later the NBC public relations department sent me another fan letter. It was from a New Jersey woman, a Mrs. Doherty, and this is a portion of what she wrote:

> **"What a magnificent Christmas tree story by Mike Leonard. He can be whimsical while weaving a story in a well-mannered, exquisite way."**

More letters followed, all forwarded to me by NBC, all signed by women, all effusive in their praise. One described a group conversation among strangers on an airplane, each of them wondering why I hadn't been given a more prominent position on the **Today** show. The writer even implored NBC to pay me more money. I couldn't believe it. My crisis of confidence was over. America loved me.

Or so I thought.

It was a Sunday afternoon. I was sitting by the fireplace with the box of fan letters at my feet. It's embarrassing to admit, but I read them often. They were filled with admiration, loaded with flattery, and overflowing with . . . underlined words. I hadn't noticed it before, but when placed side by side the pattern was unmistakable. Every sentence of every letter had three or four underlined words. Some words were underlined twice.

My mother underlines her words.

I looked at the handwriting again. There were slight differences from letter to letter, but now I was seeing them in a new light, and what I was seeing was a lame-ass amateur forgery job. All the letters in the box were clearly the work of one hand.

My mother's damn hand.

Finally, I focused on the names: Francis Sweeney, Agnes Doherty, Constance Sullivan. They rang a bell, a church bell—a church bell after a funeral. I went upstairs and looked through the stack of Mass cards my mother always sends after a friend dies. There they were: Sweeney, Doherty, Sullivan. My mother's dead friends and relatives had been used as unwitting stooges in her misguided attempt to boost my career. The charade was over. America didn't love me.

Mom did.

Margaret Marion Hattersley was born in Paterson, New Jersey, on January 8, 1922. They called her Marge. She grew up not far from my dad's house. There were three girls in my mother's family, all born nine years apart. Mom was the baby. Her father, George Hattersley, came from England and worked

The many mischievous
faces of Marge.

in Paterson's tax assessment office. Her mother, Margaret Curley, was a child of Irish immigrant parents, Martin Curley of Roscommon and Bridget O'Halloran of Cork. Martin was the proprietor of Curley's Tavern—a clean, highly regarded neighborhood bar in a working-class section of Paterson. Bridget was active in local charities but died young, at forty, from kidney disease.

Of the three Hattersley girls, Mary was the oldest. They called her Mae. She married a butcher named Jack Kelliher (see NBC phony name list), and they were never able to have children. For three decades, Mae taught music to fourth-graders at a public school in Paterson. She always felt more Irish than English and it showed on Saint Patrick's Day when Mae, decked in green, would parade her fourth-grade choral group, all wearing green sashes, into the auditorium to serenade the assembly with a stirring rendition of "Galway Bay." This routine continued until she retired, despite the fact that the ethnic makeup of Paterson had changed dramatically. In the latter years of Mae's music-teaching career the school was predominately African-American. But Saint Patrick's Day is Saint Patrick's Day. So when March seventeenth rolled around there was Mae in her green dress, once again marching her green-cloaked fourth-graders into the school auditorium. One can only imagine how bewildered the largely black audience must have been as they sat and listened to Mae's

African-American choir fill the air with the sweet lyrics of a classic Irish lament:

"If you ever go across the sea to Ireland
Then maybe at the closing of your day
You will sit and watch the moon rise over
   Claddagh
And see the sun go down on Galway Bay."

My mother's middle sister, Betty, also childless, had two tries at marriage. Her second husband was a quiet man who did some kind of work for the county. His name was Herman Diebler (see NBC phony name list), and my mom says he was a nice guy. She called him "Herman the German." Betty's first husband was a different story. He had problems. At least he did with my mother. One night she dumped a bucket of water on his head. The details are sketchy, but apparently he wasn't being nice to Betty and something had to be done. Or so Mom thought. Out came the water bucket, and the guy was a goner.

My mother is a riddle. She's a kind, thoughtful human being. She's also the first person I saw give the finger to someone. I was about six or seven. The incident stayed lodged in my memory because of the gesture's simple but powerful effect. I didn't understand its meaning, but the guy she gave it to sure did. I bet he deserved it too. My mom doesn't pick fights with strangers. She never gives waiters or store clerks a hard time. She's a generous tipper. The swear words, the wiseass remarks, the gestures—they're mostly for humorous effect. She's fishing for a laugh. Push her too far, though, and she'll push back. Some might view that as a character flaw. I'm starting to see it as her saving grace.

She isn't a fighter by nature. Somewhere along the line, however, Mom must have been forced to take a stand. She must have had to learn how to hit back. I've been around lots of people in all kinds of situations, and I've come to the conclusion that in most cases you're either a fighter or you're not. You take your lumps or you take your swings. My mother wasn't designed for combat, but she's seen it. And she survived it. Then she tried to get on with her life.

There are battle scars. They're not visible but I know she has them, rubbing away at her insides every day and every night. When the rubbing gets too painful she reacts by downing a couple of vodkas or firing off a volley of swear words, usually aimed in Dad's direction. All her present-day worries—of fiery highway collisions, of mad killers on the loose, of carcinogens in the bacon—don't quite fit with her rap sheet as a young, mischief-making prankster. Contrary forces are tough on your insides. At times I've heard my mother wonder aloud if she's crazy. I don't think she's crazy. I don't think she's a coward, ei-

Young Marge, her parents, and her
two sisters.

ther. I think she's brave. But nobody gives medals for
hiding sorrow from little boys.

My brothers and I grew up in a happy house.
Only later in life did we realize that there are a lot
fewer happy houses on Main Street, America, than
we thought. Emotional baggage is heavy. Why not
share it with somebody else in the family? Why not
pass on that anger, bitterness, and insecurity to the
next generation? Let them carry some of your load.
Mom never did that. My brothers and I never had to
carry a thing.

"Isn't there someone to check us in?" Mom asked.

"Nope," I replied. "The note on the front door just said to come on in and pick out your rooms and help yourselves to the cold drinks in the refrigerator. That's how they do things down here. At least that's how Miss Mary Lynn does things. By the way, the two of you will soon be known as 'Miss Marge' and 'Mr. Jack.' I'll be 'Mr. Mike.' That's another thing they do down here. The list is long."

We were standing inside the Bayou Teche B&B in Breaux Bridge, Louisiana, our home for the next two nights. Named after the bayou that flows behind it, the two-story wooden structure with its big front porch, five bedrooms, and backyard garden was the perfect break from RV life. We were a hundred yards or so from the main drag running through the downtown section, close enough to hear the muffled sound of tires thumping across the tall, rusty metal bridge that gives the town its name. I was hoping that we wouldn't be hearing any thumping sounds coming from the crawl space under the B&B's side entrance way. That's where Civil War fighting men supposedly hid, the scratchy handwriting of the soldiers still visible on the wood.

Breaux Bridge is the self-proclaimed Crawfish Capital of the World, but from my point of view it could just as well be called the Eccentric Character Capital of the World. Finding a character is easy. Just open the phone book. The Breaux Bridge phone directory is said to be the only one in the country to list people by their nicknames. Turn to any page, the Thibodeauxs, the Broussards, the LeBlancs, and you'll find grown men listed under "Snoopy" and "Boogie" and "Squirt." There's a "Red" and a "White" and a "Blue" and a "Black," as well as a "Big Man," a "Little Man," a "Corn Cobb," a "Toes," and a "Crip."

Marge and Crip.

I know Crip.

He works as the director of Parks & Recreation in Breaux Bridge and we became acquainted on my earlier visit. Crip is just the kind of character that I wanted my parents to meet on this trip. He's a big, jovial middle-aged man born to live up to the Cajun motto **"Laissez les bon temps rouler,"** or, "Let the good times roll." I called Crip and we hatched a plan to meet for dinner at a local restaurant and dance hall called Mulate's. He said he would bring some of his cronies and show us how the good times really did roll in Cajun country. That afternoon, while my parents and the others rested up at the Bayou Teche,

Matt and I went over to the park to find Crip and fill him in on the reason for my return to Breaux Bridge.

"Man, I'd love to do that with my parents," Crip said in his oddly metered Cajun accent, "let them see the rest of the United States. Furthest they've been is Biloxi."

I brought up the subject of Cajun nicknames.

"Everybody around here's got 'em," he said. "I been livin' here for fifty-two years and people know me as Crip. My mom calls me Crip. My teachers in high school called me Crip. Story, I'll tell you. In senior year my English teacher, Miss Moss . . . first-period . . . lady come up and said, 'Randy Cormier needs to go to the office.' My teacher said, 'We have no Randy Cormier in here.' I said, 'Miss Moss, that's me.' She said, 'Your name is Randy?' She had taught me for four years, didn't know my name was Randy."

"I never would have pegged you as a Randy," I responded. "Crip fits you better, whatever the heck 'Crip' means."

"Got the name in third grade," he explained. "Stubbed my toe and started limpin' around and my friend said I looked like that character on the TV show **Gunsmoke,** Chester, the guy with the crippled leg. From then on I was Crip."

Crip had another fellow with him. He was an older fellow, a co-worker, who was wearing a baseball cap over his white hair. His name was Ron Latoislais and when the conversation veered back to the RV trip Ron joined in, speaking in French. Crip translated:

"Enjoy your life now. The Good Lord might take you today or tomorrow. So if you need to go somewhere, go ahead and do it. Don't think about it because you might not be there tomorrow to think about it. Enjoy your life now."

Matt and I smiled in agreement, shook hands with both of them, and told Crip that we'd see him later at Mulate's.

When we arrived back at the B&B, my parents were sitting on the front porch. I suggested going for a walk through the town and they went inside to get their jackets. They didn't need jackets. It was a mild afternoon. I tried to make that point, but they ignored me. While waiting for them to come back out I started thinking about an old theory of mine. It's about people who wear coats on warm days. They are either old or crazy.

Or both.

My mother emerged dressed in her standard uniform: white floppy golf hat adorned with a haphazard pattern of orangey-tan makeup stains, a white nylon windbreaker with red and black striped sleeves, blue pants made from some kind of stretchy, fire-retardant material, nylon stockings, and white sneakers. My dad had a retirement-community cowboy thing going on. The top and bottom of his outfit, the cowboy hat and boots, were pure Western gunslinger; the middle section, a dark blue zippered jacket and pale blue polyester pants, was one hundred percent senior-citizen buffet line. The pants looked as if they had been tailored for a man two inches shorter. They were also the same pair he'd been wearing for eight straight days.

"Why the hell did you pack all those clothes?" I asked as we walked across the quiet main street toward a nearby church cemetery. "Those are the same pants you were wearing when we left Phoenix."

"Aren't they great?" he said, completely ignoring my point. "You know, I got three pairs for twenty-seven dollars and the guy who sold them to me, nice guy, he grew up in . . ."

"I've worn the same bra for ten days now."

"I really didn't need to know that," I told Mom.

"I haven't gotten the hang of that RV shower," she continued. "I've been taking French baths, dabbing myself with a soapy face cloth. I'm like a cat, licking myself clean."

"Well, the B&B has showers," I said. "Maybe you'd like to get back into that routine."

"No kidding," she replied. "My hair is a greasy mess, all pressed down. It looks like a helmet."

We walked through the cemetery gate and down a skinny sidewalk between the big stone vaults. They bury their dead aboveground in southern Louisiana, mostly because of the watery soil. Just another example of how things are different.

"Guidry, Pellerin, Boudreau, Doucet . . . ," Mom called out, reading the names on the vaults.

"No big boxes for us, Marge."

Dad was inspecting one of the big, white burial chambers.

"What do you mean?" I asked him.

"We're giving our bodies to science," he responded. "Signed the papers before we left. Might as well help people out, although once they see what they're getting they might queer the deal and send us back."

"I hope my hair is clean," my mother mumbled to herself. "Jack, you'll be giving them a good liver."

"What, Marge?"

"I said, 'You'll be giving them a good liver!' " she shouted.

And a bad ear, I thought.

We left the cemetery and walked down the main street through town. There wasn't much traffic and the sidewalks were empty. After a few blocks we ducked into a small restaurant and sat at a table near the front window. My parents ordered tea from the middle-aged waitress. I asked for a Diet Coke. We were the only customers except for an older man sitting alone in the back corner. He was dressed like a hunter and had a vaguely familiar look. I studied his tan face, his full head of white hair, and his trim white beard. Then he smiled at the waitress and his gleaming white teeth lit up the dim corner of my brain where I store scary thoughts. It was the Swamp Man, Norbert LeBlanc.

The last time I was in town, the Swamp Man had taken me out on his small boat. We floated through the mossy cyprus trees, looking for birds and other species of wildlife. He knew every inch of the swamps and every type of plant and critter that skimmed by, calling out their names in his thick Cajun accent. He was soft-spoken and funny, in a deadpan manner. I could tell he enjoyed life. Unfortunately, one of the ways he enjoyed it involved scaring the life out of me by steering his boat within inches of the huge green logs with yellow eyes. Gators. The swamp was filled with them, eyeing us from every angle. Sometimes they would sink below the surface just as we approached, bumping the bottom of the boat. Now why would that make him smile?

I told my parents about my day with the Swamp Man, then reached into a small knapsack and took out a thin spiral notebook. It contained a bunch of random observations as well as quotes from some of the more interesting people I've met on my **Today** show assignments. Norbert ranked high on that list, and I found his quote and read it to my parents:

"I raised all of my family on wildlife. We very seldom bought food. Most of the meat we had, ducks, rabbits, squirrels, deer, we never

bought that. If a man goes in the woods and starves to death he deserves to starve, you know. Because anywhere you look there's something to eat."

"Hey kids!" I whispered in a pretend voice. "Daddy's home and he's got a treat for you . . . , **Squirrel-cicles!**"

"Jeez," exclaimed my mother, "and I couldn't get you guys to eat meat loaf."

Dad gave me a look.

"Yeah, but Marge . . . ," he said.

"I know," she muttered flatly. "Cooking wasn't my thing. But you're still alive. God, all the meat loaf that went to waste."

My father gave me another look.

"We liked the canned food you cooked," I said reassuringly. "Chef Boyardee, SpaghettiOs, macaroni, TV dinners. And you did a good job with grilled cheese, hot dogs, chipped beef sandwiches, stuff like that. It's when you tried to up the ante with things like meat loaf and beef stew, that's when the trouble started."

My mother nodded her head in agreement. "I stepped out of my league," she admitted. "Boy, when we sold the house and I cleaned under the kitchen counter where you kids sat . . . I couldn't believe all the stuff that was stuck up there. I started scraping underneath and pounding on the top. Big chunks were falling to the floor. They were like bricks. Hard as stone."

Most likely, it was petrified meat loaf. And a good hunk of Hamburger Helper. Some beef stew. And more meat loaf. Cooked carrots too. More food items than I could list. We actually liked Mom's instant mashed potatoes, but they had more value when used as a kind of mortar base. We'd take a handful of mashed potatoes and smear the glob under the lip of the counter. Then we'd stick the pieces of unwanted food into the glob. There was a big radiator under the counter that burned the hell out of our knees, but it sure helped harden that mortar base. Over the years, we kept adding layers. The mixture sort of became part of whatever material the kitchen counter was made of. I bet some archeologist could analyze the layers in the petrified food chunks and figure out a time line relating to where we were in our lives. The Captain Midnight Epoch, The Bonanza Age, The Clutch Cargo Years, and then the time of mass extinctions, The Courtship of Eddie's Father Era. We crammed a lot of food into the radiator cracks too. Loose miscellaneous stuff like fish sticks, the little red things that we picked out of the TV dinners, the little brown things we picked out of the tuna casseroles—all of that stuff went into our pockets and eventually into the toilet.

I pushed away from the table and walked over to reintroduce myself to the Swamp Man, who laughingly remembered our day in the boat. I invited him to meet my parents and he sat down next to them, politely pretending to be interested as my father told him about buying three pairs of pants for twenty-seven dollars. I mentioned to Norbert that we had been discussing his Swamp & Go grocery list and then pretended to one-up him with stories of how we grew up foraging for Hostess Snow Balls.

We left the restaurant together. After saying our good-byes to the Swamp Man, my parents and I turned to walk back to the B&B. We hadn't even taken our first step when my father pivoted sharply on his pointy-toed cowboy boots and bolted back inside. Through the front window I could see him shaking the owner's hand, then walking over to where we'd been sitting to put a five-dollar bill next to the three-dollar tip that I had already left for the four-dollar restaurant tab.

"I love places like this," he gushed after coming back out. "This is what America used to be like."

"I like it too," I said. "But you have to be careful, because city people sometimes get carried away when they go to a small town. I'm not saying that about Breaux Bridge, but small towns have just as high a percentage of wackos as the big cities do. Their doors might be unlocked, but lots of times their minds are boarded shut. Everybody knows your business and if you're new to town or different in some way, you're going to have issues. I've been to hundreds of small towns because of my job and it's really easy to get caught up in the cliché of the ideal life. Stuff happens fast in the big cities and people are in a hurry. They might not have time to say hello. I think once you get past the gruff exterior, though, the nice-person ratio is just about the same. As a matter of fact, a high percentage of serial killers came from small towns."

"Oh shit," Mom muttered, looking over her shoulder.

When we got back to the Bayou Teche, I spotted Neal Angelle standing in the side yard with Kerry, Margarita, Brendan, and Matt. In his late twenties, Neal was another acquaintance from my earlier visit. He had just passed the Louisiana bar exam and was working in the Breaux Bridge branch of his uncle Randy's law practice.

"Hey Mr. Mike, how ya doin'?"

"I'm good, Neal. Are you responsible for that strange stuff on the Weber?"

"I am, sir. That's 'BOO-dan.' I thought you might want some Cajun sausage."

"Poontang?" laughed my mother.

"No, BOO-dan," he repeated, and then spelled it out. "B-o-u-d-i-n."

I introduced Neal to my parents, telling them that he was part of the big Angelle family, but then remarked how all the families in Breaux Bridge seemed big. They also seemed incredibly rooted to their ancestral home in the bayous, still able to resist the promise of a more prosperous life in a different part of the country. In the Cajun communities of southern Louisiana it's not unusual to find three generations of one family living side by side on the same street. Ask anybody about anybody else and it's a good bet that they will somehow be connected. Just take the folks I knew. The woman I called in the Visitor's Center, Jennifer Angelle, is married to Glenn Angelle, who is a first cousin to John Angelle, Neal's father. Neal's mother, Elaine, has a grandmother who is a LeBlanc and is a distant cousin to Norbert LeBlanc, the Swamp Man.

On a side note, Neal lives on the same block as the mayor of Breaux Bridge, Jack Dale Delhomme, whose cousin, Jake Delhomme, quarterbacked Carolina to the Super Bowl. Oh, and speaking of football, guess who was Neal's youth league coach? Well, what do you know, good old Crip.

"Let's go, Miss Marge. You and me."

Crip pointed to the dance floor at Mulate's, a low-slung roadside restaurant on the outskirts of Breaux Bridge. A five-piece band was playing a slow Cajun waltz as a handful of couples dressed in blue jeans and cowboy-style shirts gracefully circled the perimeter.

As Crip escorted my reluctant mother toward the band, she protested, saying that she hadn't danced in twenty years. "Well, then it's about time you did!" hollered Crip. A few seconds later, the big man in the

LSU T-shirt was teaching my mother the Cajun two-step.

Back in the dining section, Dad sat at a crowded table of men. He was talking, of course, and they were listening. They weren't just listening, they listened with genuine interest, leaning in so as not to miss a word of what he had to say. In the dim light I saw a look of sheer delight on my father's face as he spun his favorite yarns of life in a different time. Soon he too was dancing, whirling to the Cajun beat with a woman named Tina.

I stood on the edge of the dance floor, taking it all in. Tina's husband, Wayne, stood next to me. He was a friendly, middle-aged guy with an LSU baseball cap on his head. At one point, when my happy parents danced past, I looked at Wayne and smiled. He smiled back. Then, over the loud music, he leaned toward me and said, **"Laissez les bon temps rouler."**

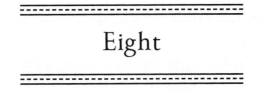

Eight

Seven-thirty in the morning and there I was again, hopping around to Cajun music. Steve Riley and the Mamou Playboys were serenading me through the earphones of my iPod as I jumped rope on a narrow wooden dock ten feet above the Bayou Teche. The song was "**La Valse du Malchanceux**," also known as "The Unlucky Waltz," but I certainly wasn't feeling unlucky, not in Cajun country.

Last night, after letting the good times roll at Mulate's, we returned to the B&B and were treated to a private concert by Jebb, Zach, and Brazos Huval, three members of a family band whom I had seen play on my earlier visit. There were fourteen kids in the Huval clan, and most were musicians with a strong interest in preserving the traditional Cajun sound. I had run into Zach at Mulate's and told him why we were in town. Before the evening was over, Zach was unpacking his accordion, Jebb his guitar, and Brazos his fiddle in the front hall of the Bayou Teche B&B.

Brazos, in his early twenties, also plays with Steve Riley and the Mamou Playboys and had just flown in that evening from the Grammy ceremonies in Los Angeles. The band was nominated but didn't win in the category of Best Traditional Folk album. Zach contacted Brazos just as he was stepping off the plane in Baton Rouge and asked him to hustle over to Breaux Bridge. All three of them certainly had better things to do on a Sunday night than to entertain a couple of elderly strangers. But there they were, playing for free and playing their hearts out.

That's what was on my mind as I jumped rope to the music of the bayous. About a hundred yards to my left was the metal bridge into town. It was a tall, rusty structure with a big red crawfish painted on the top. The bayou underneath was only about as wide as a four-lane street, its water a muddy brown. Lord knows what lived in there. Lots of crawfish, I imagined—or as the locals would say, crawdads or mudbugs. I had my own name for them: junior lobsters. That's what they looked like to me . . . from a safe distance.

I continued my rope-skipping while keeping a watchful eye for any suspicious movement along the banks of the bayou. Then I detected something. Out from the bridge's shadow came a trio of ducks paddling in my direction. I'm sure "trio" is not the correct word to describe a group of ducks, but I'm not going to pander to the radical element that insists on using the officially approved terminology such as "gaggle of geese" or "pride of lions" or "muster of storks." It was three damn ducks. Who makes up those names, anyway? A covey of dorks, I'm guessing.

The duck family was now swimming about thirty yards off. I assumed it was a family, but why just three ducks? Don't most duck families start out with seven or eight little ducklings? A chilling thought followed: The others had ended up in some gator's stomach. Or stuck on the end of a Popsicle stick in Norbert LeBlanc's freezer. As the slow-moving duck herd paddled past the dock, they heard the noise of my feet skipping against the wooden planks and looked up. Our eyes met. Prolonged eye contact has always been a challenge for me. Guilt is the probable reason. Screw-ups like me fear being exposed for what we are . . . even to ducks.

"Well, it's been over a week now, do you feel like jumping ship yet?"

Cathy was on the phone, joking about the obvious. I had finished jumping rope and was taking a break before doing my sit-ups and push-ups.

"Not yet," I answered, "but I'm afraid of getting arrested for transporting explosive material across state lines."

We laughed about some of the latest RV hijinks and I told her about our good day in Breaux Bridge. Cathy said that Megan was doing fine and it looked as if the baby would arrive close to the due date, three weeks away.

"It's still hard to believe, isn't it, Mick? Our baby is going to have a baby. How did that happen so fast?"

"Unbelievable," I sighed. "Didn't we just meet?"

Cathy O'Brien came into my life on the first day of seventh grade at Sacred Heart School in Hubbard Woods, Illinois. She was one of the new kids in the class, but her appearance made no impression on me. I was too smitten by another new student, Arnold Harper. He was a husky kid with a brush cut. At that stage of my life I valued a shortstop way more than a girlfriend. Besides, I didn't like the way Cathy looked down on me. She came from the land of the tall people. There were six kids in her family, all above average in height. Her dad was six foot four. One of her brothers grew to be six foot five. Cathy topped off at five foot nine but got there early, reaching her full adult height by seventh grade. I'm about an inch and a half taller than she is now, but my growing came late. In 1959, when our lives intersected, I was still a

TOP: Sacred Heart School dance: (left to right)
Erin Bazner, Cathy O'Brien, Jim Kauss, Mike Leonard,
Dan Gleason, and John McKechney take a popcorn break.
BOTTOM: Drunk on popcorn, Mike breaks his vow and dances.

shrimp, the third-smallest boy in the class. When the nuns lined us up to march across the street for daily Mass, they did so by height, shortest to the tallest, girls to the boys, Cathy's butt to my face.

We went to separate Catholic high schools but occasionally bumped into each other at social events. Maybe I shouldn't say "bumped into each other," because if our bodies had actually touched, Cathy would've thrown up. The standardized high school "cool guy" review sheet had just been handed out and I rated only a few percentage points above the treasurer of the Model Airplane Club. On a positive note, I was getting bigger. Unfortunately, so was my nose.

I'll tell you why.

A bunch of us had gathered for a pickup baseball game. I was in left field. My brother Jack was batting and crushed a long drive down the left-field line. I took off, my back to the infield, racing after the ball at top speed. Leaping high into the air, I stretched my left hand above my body, caught the ball backhanded, and turned my face . . . into the trunk of a tree. After regaining consciousness, my nose was broken, my lips and forehead bloodied. The mitt lay in the grass at the base of the tree. The ball was next to my foot. I had dropped the damn thing.

We finished the game and went home. Jack and I walked into the house and sat down next to Timmy at the tiny kitchen counter. Timmy always sat in the middle. My spot was to his left, wedged against the wall. Jack was positioned on the right, squished between Timmy and a red-hot burner on the kitchen stove. Kevin and my grandmother ate off TV trays in the second-floor den, soaking up the complete spectrum of 1950s television from **The Rifleman** to **Lawrence Welk**—bullets to bubbles. My parents always chowed down in the dining room, but Dad wasn't home yet, so Mom was still in the kitchen stirring a pot of Chef Boyardee ravioli. The pot was inches from Jack's right arm. Every few seconds a waft of steam blew across his face.

"What happened to your nose?" my mother inquired calmly.

"Ran into a tree," I mumbled through swollen lips.

"Oh," she said. "Well, pour yourself some milk. Dinner's almost ready."

And that was it. What's a broken nose?

About a week later, my friend Jim Kauss showed up with two borrowed tennis racquets and a can of old balls. Tennis wasn't our game, but it was mid-afternoon and there was nothing else going on. The two public courts were about a block from my house and both were occupied, so we took our seats on the bench. My bent and swollen nose was still extremely sore to the touch, but what could happen on a tennis court?

After talking for a few minutes, Jim, a fidgety lefty, got antsy and began bouncing one of the balls off his racquet, seeing how long he could keep it in the air. It wasn't long. An errant bounce caused Jim to jerk the racquet to his left, cracking the heavy wooden rim against the bridge of my tender, puffy nose, breaking it again. I lowered my head into my hands and looked down in pained silence as blood splattered off the asphalt.

A month later we were back in school. Quiet, skinny guys with big, lumpy noses don't stand a chance with teenage chicks. By early October the treasurer of the Model Airplane Club had leap-frogged ahead of me on the "cool guy" chart. Any thought of romance was put on the back burner. The one next to Jack.

High school was a drag. It wasn't the school's fault. It was mine. Back in the early 1960s Loyola Academy in Wilmette, Illinois, was run by an all-star roster of head-cracking disciplinarians. There were fifteen hundred students, none more lost than me. The teachers would finish a lesson and ask if there were any questions. I had questions about everything but was too shy to raise my hand. As everybody else plowed forward, I slipped further and further behind.

My scattered thought process only made things worse. A math teacher, trying to explain some kind of geometric shape, would ask the class to picture a slice of pie. That's what I did, but the shape would be all wrong because my mother wasn't fond of baking, so most of the pies we ate were individually wrapped

Hostess Fruit Pies, and they were sort of rectangular. That would get me thinking about other Hostess Fruit Pies—apple, cherry, lemon—and then I was gone, daydreaming about the time my brothers and I were climbing all over each other in the backseat of a station wagon bound for Florida in the late 1950s.

It seemed to take us forever to get to Miami Beach, and when we finally did arrive, so did the rain and a week-long blast of unseasonably cold air. We couldn't go swimming in the hotel pool, so my dad walked us out onto some pier to watch the fishermen. One guy had a fish on the line and was pulling it out of the water when a pelican swooped down, swallowed the fish, and started flying away. Next thing we knew the man was reeling in a bird, its wings flapping like crazy.

We never did figure out how he got the hook out of the fish in the pelican's stomach, because my dad quickly led us off the pier and across the street to a miniature golf course. On the third hole Jack and I started razzing Timmy, who retaliated by grabbing our multicolored golf balls from the dinosaur's mouth and throwing them over the fence and onto the main drag. It was kind of neat seeing the balls bouncing down the street, ricocheting this way and that off passing cars.

My father hustled us out of there and we ended up at a restaurant, where we sat in a booth next to a wiry old guy who was leaning back in his chair sucking on his teeth. My dad said something to the guy, who said something back. We got excited because it looked like there might be a fight, but then the waitress showed up with four of the biggest pieces of lemon meringue pie that we had ever seen. There must have been six inches of that white stuff on top.

Then the bell sounded. Math class was over. What does pie have to do with math, anyway?

In the spring I tried out for the freshman baseball team but didn't make it. I was still smaller than most of the other players, but that wasn't the reason for my failure. Something weird was happening to my vision, making the ball look as if it were bouncing along in the sky. I didn't say anything to the coaches or my parents because the change was subtle at first, causing me to think that the strikeouts and misjudged fly balls were just signs of a sudden, inexplicable erosion of my baseball skills.

Then came the dizzy spells. Every four or five months an unsteady feeling would hit me and the room would start to spin. A big headache would follow, and soon after that I would be throwing up. My first thought was the flu, but after a while I suspected something else. Perhaps the concussion, the croquet ball off the forehead, the collision with the tree, and a number of other whacks to the head were causing some kind of disconnect in my brain. Maybe that's why the baseballs started moving oddly. Maybe that's why simple academic concepts seemed so confusing.

Maybe I wasn't stupid, just different.

Mike in full-blown
sophomore slump at Loyola
Academy. (Slump continues
through junior and senior
years.)

These were my private thoughts. I never talked to
a doctor, a counselor, or my parents about this possible explanation for my struggles in the classroom. I
just talked to myself . . . over and over and over
again. Before long I had talked myself into believing
that failing grades didn't mean that I was going to fail
in life. In fact, it would be the opposite. So what if I
was lousy at math, English, biology, and all the other
subjects; I was good at . . . well, there wasn't anything
that I was good at, not yet, anyway. But I would find

something. Or something would find me. I convinced myself of that.

My parents talked to me about hitting the books but didn't seem overly concerned by the mediocre, and sometimes dismal, results. I never got a sense from them that a lousy high school record would condemn me to a second-rate college and a third-rate existence. They saw that I was trying, and that seemed to be enough for them.

At that time Dad was still in the marketing department at **Sports Illustrated.** The magazine was not nearly as well known as it is today. One of the perks of his job was season tickets to the Chicago Blackhawks hockey games. The seats were in the second row, a few feet from the sideboards, directly across from the visitors' bench. Chicago Stadium was a thirty-minute drive from our house in Glencoe and Dad, at our request, would get us there an hour before game time so we could absorb every bit of the rich atmosphere.

For some reason, the setting captivated me—the milky white ice, the rows of bright red wooden seats, the smell of cigar smoke, the old-fashioned boxy scoreboard, even the ceiling with its tangle of cables, beams, hanging lights, and metal catwalks. When the players glided onto the ice for the pregame warm-up I studied them in detail, noting every nuance from the scuffs on the sides of their skates to the tiny marks of wear and tear on their jerseys. What I scrutinized most closely, though, was their faces, all of them scarred, some with stitches still in place from recent wounds, others with black eyes or missing teeth.

I thought it was beautiful.

Their scarred foreheads and swollen lips weren't flaws. They were badges of honor. Every one of the players had had a rough ride to the top, and it showed. Greatness has a cost, and hockey players carry that price tag wherever they go. A missing tooth or a scarred chin was a visible reminder of the painful setbacks that achievers must endure. In the bright glow of the stadium spotlights, the toughest athletes in the world paraded their defects with pride. There were lots of bent noses. I liked that.

Our enthusiasm for the sport inspired my father to search for a recreational hockey league in a nearby suburb. Anybody could join regardless of ability, so I bought a pair of used skates and some ancient equipment at a rummage sale and reported for the evaluation session on a cold Saturday morning in November. The purpose of the gathering was to grade each person's ability, then use those parameters to balance the teams.

The outdoor rink was lined with hundreds of players waiting for their chance to impress the panel of judges. Each player would be asked to skate around a series of obstacles before shooting the puck on goal. Eavesdropped conversations told me that most of the skilled players had been at it since they were five or six years old. I was a sophomore in high school and had never played a game. With any luck they wouldn't call me onto the ice until most of the others had left. I didn't want to hear the laughter while lurching my way around the stations. The loudspeaker finally hummed to life, and the first name called was mine.

I was horrible, repeatedly losing control of the puck and myself, falling down two or three times. When the evaluation session ended, my score was one of the lowest. Yet as bad as I was, there was something about the game that felt right to me. The flow, the teamwork, even the body contact seemed to fit my personality. I could run fast. Maybe that meant that I could also learn to skate fast. The vision problem that had derailed my baseball tryout wasn't a factor on the rink, having faded away along with the dizzy spells.

A week after the tryouts, the league assigned me to a team and I stumbled my way through the first few games. It was a bad scene in more ways than one. My rummage-sale gloves must have belonged to someone's grandfather. The pants were too short, the shins guards too flimsy. I was the newest face in the oldest get-up, a 1940s movie extra who had mistakenly wandered onto the set of a present-day adventure film. The costume change was an easy fix. Switching roles was a bigger challenge. So I did something totally out of character. I set my alarm for 6:00 A.M.

That was an hour earlier than necessary, and until that moment I never did anything that wasn't necessary. Schoolwork, chores, summer jobs—none of those tasks inspired me to give anything more than what was expected of the average kid. I took comfort in that role. Nobody expected excellence. There was nothing to live up to.

When the alarm went off the next morning, my sleepy brain immediately started penning another permission slip for the normal boy to do what was normal, to roll over and drift back to sleep. It was a school day and it was still dark outside. And cold. But I shocked myself and slowly climbed out of bed.

The outdoor rink in Glencoe was five or six blocks from our house. They didn't allow hockey during regular hours, so the only way to practice was to sneak on before the facility opened. It was an open-air, natural ice rink on an empty field in the middle of a residential area. Every night at nine o'clock the park district workers would roll out the hoses and flood the surface. By morning the ice would be like glass.

Driving the family car to save time, I parked on a side street adjacent to the rink and closed the door quietly. Sound travels greater distances when it's cold. The ice surface was only about fifty yards away, but the ground was covered by four inches of crusty snow and as much as I tried to tiptoe, it sounded as if somebody were walking across a carpet of amplified walnut shells. Sitting down in a snowbank, I laced my skates, periodically exhaling great blasts of warm air into my cold, cupped hands. Then I stood up, stepped onto the ice, and glided off into the darkness.

Hockey lesson number one. Keep your head up!

It wasn't a punishing workout. No wind sprints. No shooting the puck until my hands bled. In fact, I hardly shot at all, not wanting to wake the neighbors with the sound of the puck crashing against the boards. So I just skated, moving the puck back and forth with my stick, while gliding around and around, backward and forward, turning, swooping, circling, and, most important, pretending. That's what kept me coming back—the imagined moments of glory.

My sessions wouldn't last long, thirty or forty minutes at most, followed by breakfast and school. I wasn't doing anything heroic, just a little something extra. On occasion my brothers or a neighborhood buddy, Tony Cascino, would join me. We made it fun. A few weeks later, in the third hockey game of my life, I scored three goals. That's when it dawned on me that individual achievement wasn't all that difficult to attain. Just do a little bit more.

By then Cathy had decided that it was safe to be seen with me in public. We liked spending time together, laughing and talking for hours on end, but she wasn't yet ready to glue the words "boy" and "friend" together when referring to my role in her life. I had disclosure issues as well. Being the first of my brothers to initiate voluntary contact with the enemy camp (girls) meant going underground during the initial phase of the operation. All calls to Cathy were made from discreet pay-phone locations. If I took her to a movie or met her for a meal, a fictitious reason for my absence would be given, especially to my brothers. Any time spent with a girl translated into a missed game of Wiffle Ball or driveway hockey or bottle-rocket target practice or countless other goofy Leonard-boy pastimes that kept us from maturing past the point where a church reader's mention of "the bosom of Abraham" would turn our pew into a roiling pit of uncontrollable laughter.

Mom must have known something was up, given her talent for smelling out scam artists and con men. She played it cool, though, calmly putting tin foil over my fish sticks while listening to me spin one more web of deceit about having to miss another

Friday-night dinner. My alibi boat had long been taking on water due to the flimsy wall of fabrications used to conceal my attempts at courtship. On one such occasion, a planned rendezvous with Cathy for the opening of a new James Bond movie was covered up by a leaky story about volunteering to help paint the chapel at school. It was a pitiful attempt to score goodwill points while angling for the use of the family car, but a desperate man does desperate things and out the door I went, dressed in shiny brown loafers, a clean sweater, and new pants, odd attire for a volunteer painter.

The pants felt funny, and after picking up Cathy I realized why. There was no wallet in the back pocket. This meant returning home, and since my "nongirlfriend" girlfriend hadn't been told that she didn't exist, I had to lie to her about why the car was being parked as far away from the front door as possible. Nothing was floating anymore, certainly not the pathetic fib about a colony of ants observed earlier in the day marching single file across the driveway, their sense of teamwork so impressive that . . . well, who was I to crush their spirits as well as their little bodies under the wheels of our used Pontiac Bonneville?

Mom and Dad were sitting in the living room when I raced through the front door and bounded up the stairs, calling out the reason for my return in a purposefully mumbled manner. After a few minutes of searching, the wallet was located in a pair of blue jeans balled in a pile of damp clothes muddied by an afternoon game of Smear the Queer (not queer as in homosexual, but queer as in a word that rhymes with smear). Down the stairs I raced, never planning to break stride until safely outside, when a horrifying sight caused me to decelerate too quickly. The soles of my hardly worn loafers couldn't find purchase on the waxy tile, and only because of my newly acquired ice-skating skill was I able to stay upright, skidding down the hallway, one leg kicked high, Radio City Rockette style.

Cathy was in the living room.

She had been steer-hauled from the car then bumrushed into the house by my parents. The speed and efficiency of the hostage transfer would have impressed a Delta Force commando, which Cathy wasn't. She was a seventeen-year-old Catholic schoolgirl, and the abduction had left her looking a bit shaken. Her dad and mom, Bill and Adele O'Brien, were nice, polite people, but their restrained, formal way of doing things hadn't prepared their daughter for a forced audience with Princess Whoopie Cushion and Sir Laugh-a-Lot.

The situation was dire. I had to get Cathy back into the car before Dad found the juggling balls and my younger brothers picked up the scent of a perfumed teenage intruder. Jack wasn't a worry—he had already gone out with his friend Rich Freeman, the neighborhood demolition expert, and the distant sound of a cherry-bomb explosion gave me a pretty good indication of their whereabouts. Tim and Kevin, however, were roaming somewhere in the house and would no doubt materialize within minutes, my grandmother hot on their heels.

"We have to get going," I said. "The Bond movie starts in twenty minutes and it'll be crowded."

"You're not going to paint the chapel?" Mom asked in an overly earnest way, her bullshit meter clicking loudly while her skeptical eyes locked onto my shifty gaze.

"Oh, umm, that's where we're seeing the movie . . . in the chapel . . . on a screen . . . before we paint," I replied while trying to push a confused Cathy through the front door.

"James Bond in the chapel?" Mom responded in mock surprise as I hustled toward the car.

"Hey Cath, look!" Dad yelled after us from the front stoop.

"Don't turn around," I whispered while opening the Bonneville's passenger door and shoving Cathy inside. Through the windshield we could see my father doing some kind of a soft-shoe dance on the front steps while clicking two spoons held upside down between the fingers of his right hand.

"What's going on?" Cathy asked incredulously.

"He's playing the spoons," I muttered.

"No," she said. "I mean, what just happened?"

Just then Timmy and Kevin ran out of the house

and past my dancing, spoon-playing father, shrieking my name in a girlie, singsong fashion.

"You don't want to know," I said to Cathy as the Bonneville sped away from the bizarre scene. "It would take a lifetime of explaining."

After weathering a serious amount of flak from my brothers, I began to feel somewhat liberated. An evening spent in the company of a girl no longer required the creation of alternative story lines and imaginative plot twists. Still, although greatly reduced, the specter of familial ridicule never completely disappeared, causing some problems with Cathy, who loved to dance. I didn't. It was just too dangerous. High school socials were crawling with camera-toting geeks from the yearbook staff. One click of the shutter and there I'd be, frozen in mid-watusi for all the world—and my brothers—to see and mock. So I didn't dance. Cathy went searching for boys who did.

Into the void came Mary Jo Potter, another former grammar school classmate. She was an upbeat leader in her all-girl high school, and I'm sure that some viewed her association with me as a form of intellectual slumming. The year-long linkage was good for my ego but eventually bad for my reputation as a ladies' man, the telling blow delivered with an invitation to Mary Jo's good-bye party.

"I didn't know your family was moving," I said over the phone.

"They're not," she answered.

"Then what's with the good-bye party?"

"I'm joining the convent," she replied. "I'm going to be a nun."

Yikes.

I could have tried to fill the time by hanging with the high school crowd, but for some reason my inner compass always pointed in the opposite direction from where the mainstream was headed. I didn't feel comfortable being part of a big group. It was difficult at first. The weekend nights were long and boring. Everybody else would be dancing or partying and I would be sitting at home. Then, on a summer night in the middle of my high school career, after once again pulling away from the crowd, I came upon an inspiring reason to continue searching for my role in life.

It was an outdoor folk concert at a nearby park called Ravinia, a covered band shell surrounded by a huge, grassy picnic area. Every Wednesday and Friday night during the summer months there would be a live music show and my older brother Jack and his friends would often go, mostly just to walk among the picnickers looking for a good time. One night I tagged along and as my brother and his friends headed for the grassy area, I wandered off to the band shell. The performer was someone we didn't know much about, a young singer-songwriter named Bob Dylan. He walked onto the stage alone, a six-string acoustic guitar in his hands and a harmonica holder around his neck. I leaned against a rail behind the last row of seats and watched as Dylan adjusted the microphone and tuned his guitar. Then he started to sing. Two hours later I was standing in the same spot.

Poetry had always confused me. Classic literature was incomprehensible. I was a poor writer with a limited vocabulary and no grasp of proper grammar. And yet there I was, suddenly transfixed by the power of words.

> **"And if you hear vague traces of skipping**
> **reels of rhyme**
> **To your tambourine in time, it's just a**
> **ragged clown behind**
> **I wouldn't pay it any mind**
> **It's just a shadow you're seeing that he's**
> **chasing."**

Back in the mid-1960s, Dylan had no backup musicians. His voice was crystal clear. Up until then, the only lyrics that I hummed along to were about girls or cars or surfing. Now I was hearing words that painted a whole different picture of life.

> **"Got killed by a blow, lay slain by a cane**
> **That sailed through the air and came down**
> **through the room**

**Doomed and determined to destroy all the
gentle
And she never done nothin' to William
Zanzinger."**

Before the night was over, I found myself thinking
about corrupt politicians, segregation, the arms race,
and a whole bunch of other issues that had never really concerned me. By the next day I found myself
thinking about . . . me. Maybe it wasn't such a bad
thing to be an outsider. Maybe it wasn't such a weakness to stand alone. Dylan wasn't mainstream. He
wasn't as popular as the Beach Boys or as charismatic
as Elvis. He wasn't a poster boy or a chart topper.
That didn't seem important to him.

The next morning I bought a Bob Dylan album,
then another and another. By the time school started
in the fall I knew every word from every song. I also
knew something else, something that was unde-
tectable to the people around me. They still saw the
struggling student living on the outskirts of the
high school scene, but I had already moved way past
that. I was living in the future . . . doing something
well . . . and doing it creatively. This was not just a
wish. This was a certainty. It was a monumental revelation, and it didn't come by way of a guidance
counselor or a parental lecture. It came by chance. I
had wandered away from the crowd and happened
upon a musician. The experience rearranged my psyche, giving me hope.

"For the loser now will be later to win,
  'Cause the times they are a-changin'."

Now all I had to do was find my talent, keep trying, and be patient. Patience was the key, because one
thing about me hadn't changed. I was still a slow
learner.

Nine

"Tell 'em about Touhy, Jack."

Mom sat on the RV couch, egging my father on to another reminiscent tale about their life in Paterson.

"What did you say?" asked Dad, looking up from a pile of newspapers spread out over the dinette table.

"Touhy!" my mother shouted.

"Oh, Tommy Touhy," chuckled my father, leaning back in the ejection seat. Despite a week's worth of scolding, Dad still wasn't ready to acknowledge the danger of sitting on a portable folding chair in a moving vehicle despite the sticker that warned against doing just that.

It was ten o'clock in the morning and the skies were dark. Rain had been falling since we left Breaux

Bridge a few days earlier, curtailing our plans to hit the beach in Bay St. Louis, Mississippi. I was hoping it would let up by the time we reached Montgomery, Alabama, so we could check out the city where some of the pivotal civil-rights events took place, but the rain didn't stop and neither did we. Matt had taken over the driving duties and I was in the recliner soaking up the scenery as we rolled through southern Georgia toward Atlanta.

"Tommy Touhy used to hang out at the firehouse a few doors down from where we lived," Dad said, the wooden chair teetering with each bump in the road. "We hung around there too. It was a place to gather. The firemen were good to us. They let us use the showers after our ball games and before dances. Nobody I knew had a shower at home. Tommy Touhy was always sitting in a chair tilted back against the wall."

My father tilted his chair farther back, its legs now a good two inches off the floor. One swerve of the RV and he'd be kissing the refrigerator.

"Tommy was a boxer, had maybe a hundred professional fights. He fought in the armory many times, the Paterson Armory, it was right across the street from the firehouse. Great place. There were basketball games, bicycle races, the circus—everything happened at the armory. Once a month they had boxing matches. We'd sneak in. 'Midgie' Shields would shinny up the rainspout to a walkway near the top, then climb in a window and run below to open a door for the rest of us. The main custodian, Paddy Doran, knew what was going on, but he pretended like he didn't. They should've just let us walk through the front door, but half the fun was thinking that you beat the system. Then after we got in, we'd send somebody back out again and he'd go down to 'Happy' Mahoney's store and buy a case of soda and bring it back. We would split up the cans and sell them to the people in the seats."

"The guy's name was Midgie?" I asked.

"Yeah, 'Midgie,'" Dad replied. "He was really short, so we called him 'Midgie' for 'midget.'"

I looked toward Matt in the driver's seat and he gave me the eye.

"What were we talking about?" asked Dad.

"Tommy Touhy!" shouted Mom.

"Oh yeah," he went on. "Tommy Touhy was a good fighter but he got hit a lot. He was what they call a 'catcher.' He caught a lot of shots to the head and eventually got punchy. Nice guy, though. He came over to the house all the time. My mother loved Tommy. He had a younger sister named Tilly, a beautiful girl who became a nurse. Tilly Touhy.

"Anyway, they had a clock at the firehouse with a bell on it and the thing went off every fifteen minutes. When it rang, Tommy would shoot up from the chair and throw a couple of punches at whoever happened to be next to him. It was a reflex thing. He couldn't help it. Then he'd sit back down.

"It was funny. We'd all be sitting around talking and at the same time watching the clock out of the sides of our eyes. About thirty seconds before it would ring, everybody would slowly get up and move away from Tommy. The bell would go off and he'd jump up and throw some punches at the air and then sit back down. Then we'd all move back to our chairs. Fifteen minutes later, the same routine. That went on all day long. On Christmas Eve the church would be packed for midnight Mass, not a seat left. Tommy Touhy would have a whole pew to himself. They ring a lot of bells at that Mass."

"How were those fights at the armory?" I asked.

"Oh, great," my father gushed. "Saw a lot of terrific fighters. Max Schmeling, Tony Galento, James Braddock. He was a good guy, Braddock was. Got a chance to meet him once. I was a round boy at lots of the armory fights, circling the ring with the big numbered cards after each round.

"We boxed there too, in the Golden Gloves. All the kids would sign up. It was put on by the PBA, the Police Benevolent Association, to keep everybody off the streets. They supplied two pairs of gloves and two pairs of trunks, one red and one blue. After each bout, the guys who'd just fought would come into the locker room and give the trunks and the gloves to the next two kids who were going out. On the little guys the trunks would be hanging down past their knees and on the big ones they looked like Jockey shorts. By the end of the night the stuff was soaked with sweat. The gloves would weigh a ton. You didn't want to have a bout with some tough guy at the end of the night. My friends would be whispering in my ear, saying, 'Jackie, you're gonna get the shit kicked out of you tonight.' "

My father leaned forward in his tottering folding chair and I breathed a sigh of relief. Then he laughed to himself, leaned back again, and continued reliving the danger-filled old days in a newly dangerous way.

"There was this local politician, Jake Breslin, a small-time guy, like a ward captain or something, and he was always looking for an angle. He went down to Devegas, a discount sporting goods store, and bought about eight pairs of boxing shoes in different sizes for us to use in the bouts. Before he turned them over to the organizers, though, he painted a big 'JB' on the soles of all the shoes. Then he hired a local photographer, a guy with a bum leg named Izzy Singer, to take pictures of all the fights. Izzy would be hopping around the outside of the ring, lugging the big camera and circling as fast as he could. He was hoping to be in the right position in case one of us got knocked out. Then he'd take the picture and hustle the film into the **Paterson Times** and try and talk the editor into running the shot in the next day's sports section. There one of us would be, flat on his back, a big 'JB' written on the bottom of his shoes. Breslin was smart. He got some good publicity out of it."

My son Matt was hanging on Dad's every word. If you got my dad off the subject of how the little guy keeps getting KO'd by the Tyson-esque forces of modern society, you were in for a treat. His stories were full of tiny details, oddball names, and quirky characters, all remembered with remarkable clarity. Keeping him from lurching back to the tiresome lecture series requires discipline and strategy. The best technique, not just with my father but with all interview subjects, is the assertive follow-up question. As in . . .

- What color was Tilly Touhy's hair? (Red.)
- Was Tommy Touhy married? (Yes.)
- Did he ever slug his wife by accident? (No.)
- Why not? (Because she left him.)
- Did she leave with her sanity? (Yes. And all of Tommy's money.)
- How close was your house to the fire station? (Three hundred feet.)
- Did you ever get knocked out in the Golden Gloves? (Yes.)
- How often? (Every time.)
- How early in the fight? (First round.)

Learning to jump in quickly with follow-up questions is also hugely important. My father's concentration derailments happen in the blink of an eye. Take, for example, the story about the **Paterson**

Times photo of an unconscious amateur boxer with a big "JB" painted on the soles of his shoes. That tale could instantly trigger a reroute switch in my father's brain circuitry. Before anybody realized what hit him, my father would be deep into an endless lament of how small newspapers get squashed by humongous media conglomerates. Predicting when those sudden topic detours would happen has been accomplished only a handful of times, all under tightly controlled laboratory conditions, so for now it's perfectly acceptable to bluntly interrupt him in mid-sentence. One final bit of advice for those brave enough to try this at home with their parents or grandparents: Ask small questions. They almost always lead to big answers.

"Hey Jack, I got a ham on one side." My mother had a pained look on her face and was pressing both hands against her right rib cage.

"What's the ham from?" Dad asked, paging through a newspaper.

"The damn fall I took a couple of days ago," grumbled my mother. "Remember? I didn't see that step by the bed and crashed into the dresser."

"Oh yeah," Dad nodded, still turning the pages.

Mom looked out the window and shook her head. "Shit, now the lamps are going. What next?"

"The wheels," my dad shot back, peering over his glasses. "And when the wheels go, it's curtains."

My parents were talking street again, their kind of

street, an urban lingo set down nearly a century ago yet still used on a daily basis by two Paterson, New Jersey, people who wouldn't know an etymologist from optometrist . . . or, as my parents would say, a "lamp doctor."

Eyes were "lamps." An arm was a "wing." Legs were "wheels." Large ears were "sails." All the terms were subject to exaggeration and embellishment. If a guy with big sails passed by on the sidewalk my dad might say, "Don't walk with him in a windstorm. He'd leave you in a hurry." It wasn't meant to be detrimental. It was just pointing out the obvious. The man had big ears. He knew it. You knew it. Why hide it?

Traffic was picking up as we entered the outer ring of metropolitan Atlanta. A streak of light struggled to escape from the dense, dark cloud formation.

"Hey Marge," Dad called out. "Want me to go in and get you some gum at the next gas station?"

"Yeah," she answered. "And maybe one of those granola things, the cinnamon kind."

"Bet you couldn't get a gas-station granola bar when you were growing up," I commented.

"I didn't know what the hell granola was until about five years ago," Mom replied. "Actually, I still don't know. What is it?"

"I don't know either," I answered. "Some hippie invented it. That's my guess. It's got nuts mixed in with . . . oh, who cares."

"You know what was a good invention?" Dad suddenly announced. "The tea bag."

A soggy tea bag swung from his fingers, spraying drops all over his blue pants.

"I think the first ones were made out of silk," he continued. "Paterson was called the 'Silk City,' you know. It's a shame what happened to all those jobs in the silk industry. Some big company didn't want to pay a working wage, and . . ."

The speed of that synapse shift surprised even me.

"Yeah, yeah," I interrupted. "But the tea-bag inventor should've hired a better PR firm because nobody gives him any credit, because it's called a 'tea bag,' not an 'Otto Schmeigal bag' or whatever the dude's name was who invented it."

My father shook his head and plopped the tea bag back into his cup.

"You know who got way more credit than he deserved?" I went on. "The Dopp kit inventor. Big deal, a leather bag to hold shaving stuff. I think the guy's name was Doppelt or something like that and they shortened it to Dopp, but even that gives him way too much credit. I mean, come on, it's a bag. On the other hand, the guy at 3M who invented the Post-it note, now that guy deserves his day in the sun. I did a **Today** show story on him years ago, and . . ."

"Hey Marge, remember the name of the guy who owned the gas station when we were growing up?"

Now my father was interrupting me. Have I started to become him?

"You mean 'Neck'?" my mother asked.

"Yeah, 'Neck,' " laughed my dad.

"Let me guess," Matt said. "The guy had a big neck."

"Did he ever," whistled Dad.

"Really long," added Mom. "Like a giraffe."

"You mentioned a guy named 'Happy' something when you were talking about the boxing matches earlier," I said. "I'm guessing he was always happy."

"Oh, Happy Mahoney," my father responded. "He owned the candy store. No, he was a real grouch. That's why we called him 'Happy.' "

"Makes sense," nodded Matt from the driver's seat before turning his head toward my mother on the RV couch. "But why ham?"

"You mean why did I always give Mike ham for lunch?" she asked, looking up from the road atlas, her index finger still glued to the spot she was examining.

(Note: Through four years of high school my mother never altered my daily brown-bag menu choice of two thinly sliced ham sandwiches on Wonder Bread and a bag of Fritos.)

"No, the ham on your side. Why a ham?"

"That's what we called a big lump," she explained. "A guy with a hump on his back looks like he's got a ham sitting on his shoulders, you know, like a half a ham you'd get from the grocery store. So we'd say he's got a ham on his back."

"But not to the guy with the ham, right?" asked Matt, a look of concern crossing his face.

"You would if he was your friend," crowed Dad. "He knew he had the ham. We had a kid in our neighborhood, George Bott, a good guy, his dad was a cop, Officer Bott. Well, George had some kind of deformity with his legs. They were dead. But he had crutches and he moved pretty good by leaning his body forward on the sticks, then swinging his legs to catch up. We called him 'Swinger.'"

Dad paused a bit and smiled.

"Swinger was a friend of ours and he was good to have around in case a fight broke out. His younger brother Larry was easy to beat, but not Swinger. He could really use those crutches."

Matt looked puzzled. "But who would get into a fight with a crippled guy?" he asked sympathically. "That seems kind of cruel."

"Ever get smacked with a crutch?" Dad shot back. "Hurts like hell. Swinger was unstoppable if he could find a wall to back into for support. Then he could use both crutches. You know, in fighting it's all about reach."

"So Swinger didn't mind being called Swinger," I stated in conclusion.

"No," my father forcefully responded. "It made him one of the guys. He just had bad legs. The name fit. It's not much different than calling somebody 'Lefty' or 'Red.' He couldn't help it that he had bum wheels. We weren't making fun of him. Everybody's so careful these days. When I was in grammar school, maybe about sixth grade, a nun from the principal's office came around to all of the classes and said that a new kid would be showing up the next day and he was different and we shouldn't be giving him a nickname. So the kid shows up, his last name is Reyes and he's from the Philippines. It wasn't fifteen minutes later when everybody was calling him 'Flip.' Good guy. Within a week the nuns were calling him Flip. Played all the sports, tried everything, Flip Reyes . . . loved being called Flip."

"That wouldn't go over today," I remarked. "Somebody told me about a grammar school in our area where the kids were learning to jump rope in gym class. A few kids couldn't get the hang of it, so they took all the ropes away and now the whole class jumps imaginary ropes. They didn't want the kids who couldn't jump to feel bad."

"That's crap," Dad groused. "So they can't jump rope. That's when you go over and tell them that it doesn't matter. Just give it a shot. That's all you can do. And if some kid starts laughing, make that kid run laps."

"Oh God, you can't do that," Matt said. "That's public humiliation. That's a lawsuit."

"That's bullshit," barked Mom.

The rain had finally stopped and the clouds were getting brighter by the time we reached Atlanta. Earlier in the day I had called a good friend of mine, Danny Wilson, an African-American in his early forties, who arranged to meet our mini-caravan at a truck stop, then lead us to a cohort's house where we could hang out for a bit. Danny and his friends are stylish guys with streetwise personas, so at the very least I knew my parents would come out of the experience with a few new vocabulary words and perhaps a fresh supply of hand signals to confuse and astonish even more people than usual.

Either way it would be interesting, because there aren't many people in the world like Mr. Wilson, a deeply spiritual man. He believes that our first meeting, almost fifteen years earlier, was preordained—that our very different lives intersected for a reason. I don't know what to say about that concept, other than that I find myself wondering more and more about it as the fortuitous coincidences in my life, and in the lives of people I encounter, keep piling up.

My friendship with Danny, for instance, came about because of a package that I almost threw away.

It arrived in 1990, forwarded to me by a **Today** show producer in New York. The small parcel contained a VHS tape and a letter describing the work of a young New Orleans artist named Lyndon Barrois who was using gum wrappers as his medium. Inch-high sculptures made of discarded gum wrappers weren't causing much of a stir in the art world, so the **Today** show producers sent the proposal to me for final burial.

Procrastination kept the small package hidden

under a pile of paperwork on my desk. Months later, while cleaning up the mess, I found the packet and was about to toss it, thinking it had become dated material. But I didn't, and after reading the first few paragraphs of the letter my thoughts started focusing more on the writer than on the person he was writing about. Why would this guy go to all that trouble trying to engineer a break for his friend when there was nothing in it for him? And who did he think would show interest? National news organizations don't expend time and money to shine a spotlight on a couple of young, unknown black men, one of them doing art that wasn't yet considered art and the other . . . who knows what the other guy's story was?

A thought interrupted my reading. It centered on something that happened earlier in my life. I had been in my late twenties, with a wife and three young children. We were just scraping by when a friend of mine came to our rescue. His encouragement gave me the strength to press on when things looked bleak. Without his help, I wouldn't have made it in television.

Turning my attention back to the New Orleans artist and his letter-writing friend, I put off watching the videotape and dialed the number on the bottom of the page; Danny Wilson answered. A week later he was standing next to me in a humble New Orleans home, while a camera crew focused its attention on a collection of tiny gum wrappers, brought to life by his best friend, Lyndon.

Back then the inner wrapping on a stick of gum was made of foil, and that's what Lyndon used for his minuscule sculptures, a ready supply always at hand thanks to Sylvia, his gum-chewing mom. Lyndon twisted the foil into human forms, painted them in fine detail, then arranged the figures to depict an action-filled sports scenario. The incredibly intricate process was Lyndon's passion. He was making something out of nothing, turning little scraps of trash into what he and his friend Danny considered art.

The story aired on the **Today** show in October of 1990, and soon afterward Lyndon telephoned to thank me for exposing his work to a national audience. The response shocked him. Calls were coming in from everywhere. The company behind **Ripley's Believe It or Not** commissioned fifteen of his works to be exhibited in different parts of the country. The money was good, and Lyndon started saving the unexpected income for something else that he had been dreaming about—animation school.

Meanwhile, Danny kept hoping that his internship at a New Orleans PBS station would lead to a break of his own. The odds of making it in any creative field are always long, or so they say. Danny and Lyndon ignored what the odds-makers were saying. So did I. As the years went by, the three of us stayed in touch. Lyndon invited me to his wedding. Danny did the same.

The entrance to the truck stop was a mile ahead on the right. It had been nearly fifteen years since Danny Wilson's package arrived in the mail. Much has happened since. Danny's internship with the PBS station did, in fact, lead to a job as a TV cameraman in Minneapolis, but budget cutbacks put him out of work. He scrambled to his feet and found something at a radio station, and from there he went into event production. The days were long and the pay was relatively low, but Danny kept pushing hard and staying positive.

It paid off. Honest diligence was rewarded with a position as road manager for big-time music stars ranging from LL Cool J to Jay-Z. The wear and tear of travel, however, started to get to him, and he was considering other options when a friend invited him to listen to a new form of music. That, says Danny, is the day he discovered why he was put on this earth.

"Mr. Wilson," I said after hugging my friend hello, "I'd like you to meet my mom and dad."

"Hi Mom, I'm Danny Wilson."

The tall, slender man in the blue baseball cap gave my mother a big hug and then moved down the center aisle of the Holiday Rambler to shake hands with my father.

"Hello Dad, nice to meet you, sir."

Now in his early forties, Danny Wilson is a happily married father of a piano-playing daughter. He's also the general manager of an Atlanta radio station and one of the founders of Holy Hip-Hop Holdings, Inc., a conglomeration of video, radio, Internet, and print outlets formed to spread a genre of music that combines hip-hop music with positive lyrics.

As for Lyndon, well, he actually did make it to animation school . . . and way beyond. In addition to an impressive list of TV and film credits, Lyndon Barrois, the young man who saw artistic value in a wastepaper basket full of gum wrappers, became the animation supervisor for all the battle scenes in the blockbuster movies **Matrix Reloaded** and **Matrix Revolutions.**

"Come on, everybody," called Danny from the interior of the Holiday Rambler. "I'd like to introduce you to my friend Terrell. He's a producer here in Atlanta who's been working with us on some Holy Hip Hop concert videos. He's got an editing studio here in his house, and I thought that would be the best place to give you a taste of what we're doing."

The RVs were parked on a cul-de-sac in front of Terrell Taylor's big home in an upscale Atlanta suburb. The scheme that Danny and I had concocted involved sitting my parents in front of one of Terrell's huge video monitors, cueing up some scene of a hip-hopping brother in a sideways baseball hat, then cranking the volume and watching my mom and dad squirm. I knew that common courtesy would prevent my parents from making a scene, but I guaranteed Danny that their struggle to stay composed would be a sight in itself.

As my parents and the rest of our traveling party stepped down from the RVs and introduced themselves to Terrell and his cousin C-Dash, Danny pulled me aside to comment on something in my dad's wardrobe that clashed mightily with the rest of his "standard-old-guy outfit."

"That blue cap," Danny half whispered. "When I first saw it I said to myself, 'No, it couldn't be.' But then your dad turned and I saw that it was a Kangol and I was like, 'My man is cool.'"

Kangol-brand hats still carried some weight in black neighborhoods. I don't know when or where my father purchased his, a dark blue cap with the small Kangol kangaroo logo on the back, but I did know this: The man had no clue at the time of purchase that his street rep was about to skyrocket. Just to hear Danny's reaction, I asked if he thought my father had any inkling that he was strolling down Cool Street.

"No!" he shouted. "No, he don't know. But he is. He's mad cool."

While Terrell ushered my parents and the rest of the group into the side entrance leading to his editing room, Danny and I stayed outside for a couple of minutes so I could fill him in on how our journey had come about. I told him about my dad's ups and downs and how my parents were never able to amass a big enough nest egg to retire in style. Danny's a good man, one of the best I have met. He understands struggle. To him, a rich legacy has nothing to do with being rich.

"I think society connects everything to material things," Danny said softly. "But if you look deep down in your heart, if I was a good person, if I treated people nice, you know, if I was well respected in school, those are the things that make you feel that I had a good life, whether I had a million dollars or one dollar."

"You're right," I replied. "But that philosophy doesn't fit with how success is measured today. How many mainstream hip-hop videos do you see where somebody's not showing off their fancy car, or huge mansion, or gold teeth?"

"I know," he nodded, before summing it all up with brilliant simplicity. "Life is easy." He sighed. "We make it hard."

Terrell had the concert footage ready to go when we joined the group in the studio. My parents had taken their seats in front of the big television monitor while the rest sat in chairs scattered behind them.

"Hey Danny," I said. "Give my parents a little background on what kind of music they're about to hear."

"Puff Daddy?" Mom asked.

"Close," laughed Danny. "This type of music was called rap a few years ago, but now most people use the term 'hip-hop.' It came out of the same culture, though, and the popularity really grew when budgets were cut and they started taking musical instruments out of schools. The kids made their own form of music, scratching with records, break dancing, and spinning on the ground. Hip-hop is a form of self-expression. Holy Hip Hop is the same, except it's got spiritual lyrics over hip-hop beats. It's an alternative, a way for people to hear positive messages without having to, uh, you know . . ."

"Give up their beat?" Dad suggested.

Danny's exaggerated double take cracked up everybody in the room.

"Yeah!" Danny shouted. "Don't have to give up their beat. Give me a pound. You know what a pound is?"

"Sure," Dad replied, extending his closed fist toward Danny. "It means 'shake hands.' "

"See, he knows!" Danny screamed. "He knows!"

Then the music started, and whatever Dad knew went streaking out the window. A look of utter bafflement radiated through his transparent attempt to appear riveted by the lyrics. For all my dad really knew, or my mom, the hip-hopper could have been shouting out his rhymes in Finnish. To make matters worse, my dad started bopping his head to the beat, or to be more accurate, to **a** beat, because it clearly wasn't **the** beat. Behind him my kids were doubled up, their shrieks of laughter camouflaged by the blaring music. The song's final notes, like the dying whine of a dentist's drill, brought a sudden flow of color back to my parents' faces.

"I liked his jewelry," Mom lied.

"Yeah, his ice," Danny nodded. "That's a term for jewelry. Like if I say, 'Mrs. Leonard, you're iced up,' it means I like all your jewelry."

Mom turned to Dad. "Hey Jack," she blurted. "I want some ice for Valentine's Day."

That brought another round of laughter and new bellowing from Danny.

The Holy Hip-Hop Tour:
(left to right) Danny Wilson,
Marge, Mike, Jack, Terrell
Taylor, and C-Dash.

"Word!" he cried, followed by a quick translation. "That means 'I agree with you.' Word."

After a few more minutes of small talk, we made our way back to the RVs and bid Danny and his friends farewell. My parents took their seats on the couch and waved out the side window to Danny, Terrell, and C-Dash as we pulled away.

After a few minutes in quiet thought, my mother's expression suddenly grew into one of puzzlement.

"Hey Jack," she asked. "When they say 'word,' it's the same as saying you agree with them, right?"

"Yeah," he nodded. "Like if I gave you a bite of my sandwich and asked if you liked it, you would say, 'word.'"

"Well, what's the point?" my mother continued. "Why don't they just say 'fine'? That's only one word."

"Hell if I know," Dad replied, scratching his head.

The campground in Winder, Georgia, wasn't far away and on the drive over I brought up the perplexing concepts of coincidence, luck, intuition, and whether or not God has a plan for our lives.

"I don't think we're supposed to know those answers," my father replied.

"But certain situations sure do make you wonder," I added. "During a **Today** show trip to Iowa about ten years ago I passed by a monastery in a small town and had some free time, so I decided to check it out, never telling the people in the visitor's center that I worked for NBC. I just wanted to see if there were any story possibilities. A lot of the monks had taken the vow of silence and were out working in the fields. They grew their own food at the monastery and sold some of it in a cafeteria open to the public. There was also a small gift shop, and I went in to look around. While thumbing through one of the books for sale a voice came out of nowhere.

" 'Are ya Irish?'

"On a stool in a back corner of the shop sat an ancient monk; he must have been in his nineties. He looked like a mummy. I walked over to him.

" 'Are ya Irish?' he repeated. " 'You look so to me.'

" 'Well, my ancestry is Irish,' I answered. 'I'm taking a guess that you are.'

" 'I am,' he said. 'Came here from Tipperary.'

" 'Ever been back?' I asked.

"He gave me an incredulous look.

" 'I haven't been beyond the monastery's front gates since I arrived when I was seventeen.'

" 'Would you like to go back?' I continued.

" 'Oh,' he sighed. 'I would love to go back but I can't. This is where God wants me to be and this is where I will die.'

" 'So where in Tipperary are you from?' I quizzed. 'I've been all over that county.'

" 'Not to my village,' he chuckled. 'Nobody's been there. It's tiny. No tourists at all.'

" 'What's the name of it?' I pressed.

" 'It's called Fethard,' he said, then slowly spelled the name."

My parents were listening intently. At this stage of the story I paused to give them some details about my NBC trip to Ireland in 1982, relating how I would often drive through the countryside alone, bringing along my home video camera in case something of interest arose.

Then I returned to the tale of my encounter with the ancient monk.

"So after he told me he was from Fethard, I looked down at him on the stool and said, 'Not only have I heard of Fethard . . . I've been to Fethard.'

"The monk sat there in silence, then raised his eyes to mine and asked in a half whisper, 'What's it like?'

" 'Just the way you remember it,' I answered, knowing how certain parts of rural Ireland resisted change. 'In fact, you're not going to believe this, but you can see for yourself. I took home movies of your village: the church, the main road through town, the cemetery, the shops . . .' rattling off a partial list of shots that came to mind.

"The old monk seemed dumbfounded as I described traveling through dozens of other small villages during my ten days in Ireland, most of them far prettier and more historic than his birthplace. Fethard, however, was the only place where I felt compelled to walk back to where I parked the rental car, unpack the video camera, and take not just a few shots, but ten minutes of video from every angle.

"As he continued to sit in speechless silence, I promised to send him a copy of that tape and then explained how he could see his hometown on a TV screen if someone from the monastery could arrange to borrow a VHS machine. After getting back home, I looked through my old videos, found the tape of Fethard, and sent a dub of it off in the mail.

"Well, months later a handwritten letter arrived from the Iowa monk. It was written in scrawled pen and it was short. He wished me well. Then, at the end of the note the old monk wrote about how blessed his life had been. He said that God had answered all of his prayers, especially the last one, about returning to his hometown in Ireland just once before he died."

My parents sat and stared.

"Kind of a cool story, huh?" I said, just to break the quiet.

My mother's response was short.

"Word."

Ten

"Two more weeks, Meg."

"I know, Dad, it's crazy, isn't it?"

I spoke on the cell phone with my daughter while steering the Holiday Rambler through the Blue Ridge Mountains of North Carolina. Behind me and to the right, positioned sideways on the couch, feet up, hands folded, a halo of serenity backlighting her mix-mastered red hair, sat my mother . . . quietly. The sight of a cell phone anywhere near the steering wheel usually triggered a blizzard of four-letter words. But now she was calm. The climate is wildly unpredictable in MargeWorld.

"So Meg," I continued, "any inkling of whether it's going to be a boy or a girl?"

"I think it's a boy," she answered. "You and mom had Matt first, Jamie was born before Marcy, Moose had all boys—I just think it's going to be a boy but I don't care either way."

"Are you glad that you don't know?"

"Yeah. Mom says that you can count on two things during labor and delivery: pain and surprise. Why would you get rid of the good one? So where did you guys sleep last night?"

"Oh man," I replied. "Last night was spooky. We camped in the middle of the woods . . . some state park in Georgia. It's the off season, so it was just the two RVs surrounded by a pitch-black forest."

"Was Moose freaking out?" asked Megan.

"Hey Moose!" I yelled, turning slightly in her direction while keeping my eyes on the winding road. "Megan wants to know what you thought of last night's campground."

"It sucked," my mother responded pleasantly while admiring the mountain views. "I was scared shitless."

"She liked it," I joked to Megan before lowering my voice to fill her in on the details of our nighttime arrival. "You should have heard her when we were driving through the woods looking for our campsite. We had to go slowly to try and see the numbers. At one point she let out this little scream and cried, 'Oh God, there's a bear behind those bushes. It's staring at us. And it's got babies with it.' I thought the detail about the babies was great, even though it was a bunch of crap. A few minutes later she said she saw a pistol range. With somebody on it!"

"A pistol range?" laughed Megan. "In the woods? But it was . . ."

"She didn't see any pistol range. Or a bear with babies. She just wanted us to be as scared as she was."

"Were you scared?"

"Hell yeah," I quickly responded. "Come on, we're Leonards. Darkness plus wooded areas always equals heart failure. We ate together in the Holiday Rambler and then split up and barricaded ourselves in for the night. I don't think any of us slept very well. It was the perfect setting for a horror movie—a family of campers alone in the woods. Cue the inbred dude with an ax, or the crazed animal, or the alien, or the Mummy."

"I thought you were okay with the Mummy," questioned Megan. "You know, according to that ratings system that you and your brothers had."

"Oh, the Top Four Monster List," I replied, happy that Megan remembered some of the childhood stories I had told. Rating the movie monsters using athletic criteria was an ongoing Leonard-boy diversion.

"Yeah, I shouldn't have mentioned the Mummy. He wasn't that scary to us; that's why he never got above number three. Lack of speed hurt him. He had to drag that bum leg and all those bandages around."

"Why was he even on the list?"

"Because he was always on TV. There was a show on Friday night called **Shock Theater** and they played the four monsters in heavy rotation, kind of like music on mainstream radio. The Mummy had two things going for him: thousands of years of experience and a great choke hold. His victims were suckers, though. They just froze and let him strangle them. All they had to do was throw a head fake and take off.

"We had Frankenstein ranked at number two. He was really slow too, and dumber than shit, but we rated him higher than the Mummy because of his unbelievable strength. And he looked cool with the flat head, the bolts in the neck, the scar, the striped T-shirt under the sport coat, the tight pants, the big boots. He had monster style."

"And Dracula wasn't . . ." Megan began.

"Dracula was a pansy," I blurted out. "I mean, the guy wore a tuxedo. He looked like a waiter. Plus, his hair was greasy, he had long fingernails, it looked like he wore lipstick, and he was way too polite. Sucking blood and turning into a bat didn't even come close to making up for those weaknesses. And the crucifix thing . . . going to a Catholic grammar school there were crucifixes everywhere. He could never get within ten feet of us. That's why Dracula came in last."

I could tell that Meg was enjoying the conversation. We did this a lot as a family, taking a silly topic and discussing it at length in serious tones. It was a funny way to stay connected with the kids.

"So . . . ," concluded Megan, "the Wolfman was number one."

"No, no, not the Wolfman," I said, "The Werewolf. There's a big difference. We felt they overdid it with the Wolfman. They actually made him too furry. There was something else that really bothered us about him: He was kind of nerdy. He always looked troubled, almost like he felt bad for killing people. But what killed him for us was the weight issue. He was a little chubby. A wolf has to be able to run, that's just part of the deal, and it was clear to us that this guy hadn't been putting in the miles. So we disqualified him. The Werewolf, on the other hand, had it all with the slanted eyes, sharp teeth, just the right amount of fur, world-class speed, good physique, could either bite or claw you to death . . . He was the real deal. They don't make them like the Werewolf anymore. Once Linda Blair started puking, the monster game changed forever."

"I must have had some Linda Blair in me," Megan laughed.

"You did!" I exclaimed. "For one thing, you were born the same year **The Exorcist** came out, 1973, and two, you puked like it was your job that first year. Mom and I had to develop quick reflexes just to stay dry. One second you'd be fine, all smiles in the high chair, then without warning a geyser of Blueberry Buckle would be shooting toward us. We were like those groundhogs in the arcade game, ducking in and out of the holes to avoid the mallet . . . the barf mallet."

"And the car, what were the details about that . . . ?"

"Oh Megan, we bought that big damn station wagon in the middle of the gas shortage because you puked all over the backseat during the test drive. Twice! On the same ride! We never intended to buy the thing. It was a fuel hog. Everybody was moving to smaller cars. The salesman was working to unload it on us because we were young and naïve. He pressured us into taking it out for a spin. I was driving, and the salesman was sitting in front with me. You and Mom were in the backseat. I think Matt was with my parents. About two minutes into the drive I heard that awful sound of barf hitting vinyl. Cathy's apologizing while mopping up the backseat with a diaper . . . when you blow again. The guy got pissed. We brought the car back to the dealership, and while Cathy finished wiping the barf up I signed the papers. Drove it home that night. Never even got a chance to enjoy the new-car smell. You were about three months old. We called you 'Chatty Pukie' after the 'Chatty Cathy' doll. Pull the string on your neck and instead of words coming out, it was vomit."

Megan laughed again. "Yeah, Mom told me that I

was a costly barfer. I would never just upchuck on the floor. It always somehow hit a library book or something like that. I suppose if there's any justice in the world, my baby will be a barfer too."

"Ah, but a cute barfer, Meg. Where's Jamie?"

"He's fixing up the baby's room. It's all painted, the crib is set up, just a few more things to do. I better go help him. See ya, Dad."

"See ya, Meg. Call me if anything happens."

Just as I was closing the cell phone, Mom's voice rang out from the RV couch.

"Remember when I brought the fake vomit to church?"

Any mention of the word "vomit" usually triggered a giggle from my mother. Matt heard Mom's question and her laugh and was immediately intrigued. "What fake vomit?" he asked.

"Oh God," she giggled again. "Mike knows. He was there with his brothers. It was eleven o'clock Mass. The place was packed. Jack had brought some fake rubber vomit home from a business trip. It was when that stuff first came out, so nobody in our neighborhood had seen it yet. I put it in my purse. When we got to Sacred Heart, Mr. Corbett was one of the ushers. He was a nice guy but really serious about the ushering, so I knew I had a good mark. Well, just as the Mass was ending I tossed the rubber vomit onto the floor by the foot of that marble holy-water stand in the back of church. Nobody saw me do it. Then I went up to Corbett and told him that I smelled something funny when I went to bless myself. He came over and freaked out." My mother started giggling harder.

"Yeah, Corbett was pissed," Dad piped in from across the RV. "He was in a hurry to go someplace, and now he had to find the bucket and the mop."

"Well, he goes and gets the mop and fills the bucket with water," continued Mom, "and you guys were great, standing there looking real serious, never letting on to anybody. Corbett finally wheels the big bucket over to the rubber vomit and before he tries to mop it up he stares at Kevin, who was about five, and says, 'It was him. I know it was him. Look how pale he is.'"

Now my mother was really laughing, barely able to choke out two or three words in succession.

"And . . . it . . . was . . . true," she sputtered. "He . . . was . . . pale . . . because . . . he . . . was . . . always . . . getting sick. But . . . not . . . then."

She had now reached the highest plane on the laughter scale, the breathlessly silent zone.

"So Corbett takes the wet mop out of the bucket," my dad chimed in, "and when he tries to mop up the vomit, it just keeps moving across the floor. That's when you and your brothers started to lose it."

Mom was doubled over, wiping her eyes with one hand and pounding her thigh with the other.

"Why did the funniest stuff happen in church?" I

called out to no one in particular. "I suppose it's because you're not supposed to laugh. But how could
you not laugh watching those old-guy ushers try to
chase down that big, hairless dog that Jack sometimes
let in? And then the bird."

"Didn't you do something with a rope?" Matt
asked.

"Oh yeah," I nodded with a smile. "It was a short
velvety rope with brass hooks on each end. They
hooked it between the two communion rails right in
front of the altar. The kids who were communion
servers sat in the first row back then and at a certain
point in the Mass they got up, walked to the rope,
unhooked it so they could get to the altar, and then
refastened it to keep the altar separated from the con-
gregation. Well, Jack and I got to church early one
day, unhooked one end of the rope, and twisted it in
our hands a million times so it was really coiled and
tight. Then we struggled . . . it took both of us . . . to
hook it back on. We sat way up front that day. It was
unbelievable. The communion server was probably a
fifth-grader, so his hands weren't that big or strong.
He struggled to unhook it at first because it was so
tight, but when he finally did get the hook off the
ring the rope kind of made a noise like 'zzzzzzzzz'
and leaped out of his hand, spinning wildly. Jack and
I were crying."

"What's wrong with us?" Mom wheezed, dabbing
her eyes. "We're all going to hell."

"And you were complaining about the heat in Phoenix," Dad muttered.

It was early afternoon when we drove the RVs onto the grounds of the Biltmore Estate in Asheville, North Carolina. Given their humble beginnings, I thought it would be interesting for my parents to spend part of a day wandering around the largest private residence in the country. Built on 125,000 acres and opened in 1895, the gigantic house served as a country getaway for George and Edith Vanderbilt and their young daughter Cornelia. The brochure didn't say if Cornelia was a barfing baby, but when a family of three has forty to fifty full-time servants and over four hundred others working to maintain the property, it's safe to assume that George and Edith never played rock, paper, scissors to see who would mop up little Cornelia's barf.

"Can you imagine getting this kind of free pass just for opening your eyes?" My father was peering through the front window of the RV as we turned the last corner on the three-and-a-half-mile driveway and caught our first head-on glimpse of the mind-boggling, 250-room mansion.

"Just for opening his eyes," he repeated, shaking his head in wonder.

George Vanderbilt's eye-popping wealth came via steamship and railroad car, the two industries that grandpappy Cornelius Vanderbilt built, largely on the backs of cheap immigrant labor. The Biltmore Estate, now owned by the Vanderbilt heirs, is one of North Carolina's most popular tourist attractions. Years ago, I did a **Today** show story on the mundane hassles of spring cleaning, using the Biltmore House as a ridiculously large example. ("Honey, I'm going up to clean the gutters. I'll see you at the end of summer.")

As with many of my stories, I became friends with someone on the scene, in this case Elizabeth Sims of the Biltmore's marketing staff, and we stayed in touch through the years. When I saw that our route would take us near Asheville, I called Elizabeth and asked if we could swing by. She welcomed the idea and laughed when I described the visual of the two RVs pulling up to the colossal front entrance. ("Mr. Vanderbilt, sir, the Clampetts have arrived. Shall I broom them off before allowing them in?")

Elizabeth met me with a hug, and after introducing her to my parents and the rest of the group we walked into the house and began our abbreviated tour. It was late afternoon and the last public showing had ended, so the place was ours.

"Everything that you see in the house is original," Elizabeth announced, guiding us through the front hall's massive stone archways and then over to George's male-bonding wing. There was a billiard room, a smoking room, and a gun room. I didn't see any pole-dancing apparatus, however.

"Holy shit!" exclaimed Kerry as we walked into the banquet hall. The ceiling was seventy feet high. The table had sixty some chairs. There were Flemish tapestries, flags, animal heads, statues, woodcarvings, and a triple fireplace at one end.

"Hey Marge, let's have a dinner party," Dad suggested.

"Yeah," Mom answered. "Call Chef Boyardee."

Most people in the real-estate business quantify the size of a home's living area in square footage. The Biltmore folks measure theirs in acres. Imagine heating, cooling, or—worse—furnishing a house with four and a half acres of interior space. Someone calculated that you could actually fit a subdivision of eighty-eight average American homes inside the Biltmore House. But no ceramic lawn ornaments. They don't work with the Flemish tapestry.

We marched on, gawking at the sixty-five fireplaces, the rare art, the bowling alley, the thirty-some family and guest bedrooms, the three kitchens, the indoor pool.

"They had thirty-four bathrooms at a time when bathrooms were not the norm in the mountains of North Carolina," Elizabeth explained as we entered George's bedroom suite. "The walls in here are gold, brushed on burlap."

I glanced at my mother and saw that funny look in her eye.

"You can bet there was a lot of hanky-panky," she giggled.

George and Edith, by the way, had separate bedrooms. Maybe he was a snorer.

He certainly was a reader. Over ten thousand books line the polished wood shelves of his personal library. The shelves are on two levels, connected by a magnificent spiral staircase. A quick survey of the titles didn't impress me. Not one Hardy Boy book. There was lots of art, though: busts of smart-looking people and on the ceiling, a massive painting of a morning sky filled with angels. If the intent was to make the viewer feel small, it worked. Matt must have shared the same impression, because he pointed to an immense globe standing in the corner of the room, then turned to me and mouthed the words "actual size."

As we walked from room to room, everybody in our group was dumbstruck by the splendor that surrounded us, although at times my father appeared preoccupied, almost agitated. In a gigantic hall dominated by framed paintings of various Vanderbilts, he shuffled over to my side and leaned in close.

"My mother used to work in a place like this," he whispered.

My father's mother, Annie Smith, left Ireland as a teenager to work in the household of a wealthy New Jersey family. They treated her well, but she knew her place in the world. She was working class. That was her lineage. An immigrant girl minus a grammar-school diploma doesn't have much of a say in how she's viewed by the guardians of the social order.

But those people never asked her son, my father, to speak on her behalf. So that's what he does now. Every chance he gets.

Annie Smith on her wedding day.

Since the trip began, not a day has passed without a mention of Annie. We heard about her kindness, her compassion, and her strength. And when he talked about Annie, he talked of his father, Tom—how hard he worked, how much he sacrificed, what he went through to make life better for his children. They had their faults—he sometimes drank too much, she was on occasion too timid—but the disagreeable moments, and there had to have been some, have been whitewashed by the years, the absence, and, most important, by the realization that everybody gets walloped along the way—the Smiths, the Leonards, even the Vanderbilts. How people deal with those wallops, how they cover up the bruising and compensate for the pain, is where life gets complicated. Once you learn how someone got whacked, or where, or why, you begin to see him or her in a new light. You understand where their wackiness came from.

"P. Diddy should see this place," Mom cracked as we walked outside. "He might want to build one just like it."

"Would you knock it off with this Piffy guy?" Dad groaned. "Who the hell is he and why do you keep talking about him?"

"I just like his name," she laughed. "And I like watching you get pissed off."

Marge, Jack, and Mike
moments after deciding NOT
to purchase The Biltmore Estate
in Asheville, North Carolina.

We had finished the tour and were walking to the far edge of a side garden where we could view the back of the mansion and a good portion of the eight thousand acres that are still part of the property. Elizabeth had to take care of some quick business, so we sat outside and waited for her to return.

"Can you imagine what kind of Wiffle Ball stadium you could build here?" I asked, eyeing the huge expanse of flat, treeless space adjacent to the mansion.

"But they weren't ballplayers," Dad muttered. "Did you see the paintings?"

"Yeah," Brendan nodded. "The guy looked spazzy."

"Sometimes I kind of feel sorry for rich people," Mom added. "They don't seem happy."

Dad took off his hat and scratched his head. Dozens of chimneys sprouted from the huge roof behind him. "You make your own happiness," he said. "You don't buy it. My father had ten dollars when he landed, and ten dollars doesn't get you very far when you've got a second-grade education. Not even in the year 1900."

"How did he end up in New Jersey?" Margarita asked.

"Well, he somehow found his way to a boarding house in New York City, then heard that there might be work in Jersey City. He went there and got a job on a trolley car. They gave him a uniform coat with shiny brass buttons. Wearing it made him feel important. When he pulled the cord and rang the bell the riders took notice. It sounds silly, but if you're a lonely nineteen-year-old farm boy in a new country it's a big deal when people notice you. But then he goofed up somehow and got fired. His status was gone. 'They took me buttons,' is how he phrased it.

"Back then there was a lot happening in Paterson, a lot of industry," Dad went on. "They used to call it the Silk City because so much of the silk used in America came from the mills in Paterson. They made other things too, locomotive engines, pistols . . . all kinds of things. Most of those jobs were for skilled workers and my dad didn't have a trade, so he did what the other Irish did and tried to get on the payroll as a cop or a fireman, but there were no spots available. He got lucky, though. Somebody gave him a shovel and told him to start digging. That's how he got his job with the New York Telephone Company."

"How long did he stay there?" Brendan inquired.

"Until he retired. They kept him working right through the Depression. Didn't pay him with cash, it was scrip that he could trade for food and other things, but only at certain stores. Eventually he became a supervisor. Nobody could ever say a bad word about the phone company in his presence. He was a company man. Anything they said, he did."

"Did he climb the poles?" I asked.

"Oh yeah," Dad said with enthusiasm. "He did anything. One time there was a break in a telephone line that ran along the top of a five-foot-wide underground water pipe. They had no idea where the line was broken. The only way to find and fix it was to send someone into the pipe. So they asked my father.

"The water level was lowered halfway and a makeshift wooden raft was built, with a lantern attached to one end. They put my father on the raft, lying face up, handed him some tools, then shoved him into the pipe."

"God, how scary would that be?" Matt cried.

"And dark . . . and claustrophobic," I added.

"They told him to push himself along until he found the break," Dad continued, "then fix it, and keep pushing until he came out the other end. The other end was five miles away."

Everybody groaned at once. It was a weird story to hear as the late afternoon sun dipped below the mansion's roof, adding even more length to the enormous shadow of the Vanderbilts' wealth.

"My dad did what he was told and prayed that someone wouldn't forget that he was in there and raise the water level. He finally found the break, patched it up, and came floating out the other end of the pipe. There was a local newspaperman there and he asked my dad why he agreed to do it. 'It's me job' is all he said."

"Man, I'd quit first," said Matt.

"No you wouldn't," replied Dad. "Not if you couldn't get another job."

"How did your parents meet?" asked Margarita.

"I'm not sure," Dad replied. "Probably at one of

those social gatherings for Irish immigrants. They were married in St. Bridget's Church and eventually moved into the house on Pennington Street, the house I grew up in. My dad bought it for $4,000 and sold it twenty-five years later for $4,000. Thought it was the greatest deal anybody every made—'We lived all those years for free' is how he put it. Of course, he put a lot of work into it, put in the steam heat, the hardwood floors, the electricity, the copper gutters. He made a garden in the back. We had the top two floors and rented out the bottom. Thirty-five dollars a month.

"During the Depression, a man and his wife lived on the first floor. He lost his job and couldn't pay the rent. One day I heard my father say, 'Annie, I think I'll knock on the man's door and ask him when he thinks he can pay.' My mom got mad and said, 'Don't you be knocking on anybody's door when they're havin' trouble. The poor man can't help it.' People today don't realize how bad it was during those years. You just can't imagine."

"I read that a lot of people killed themselves," I said. "Did you know any?"

"I knew of them, sure, you were always hearing about it, but it really wasn't people we associated with. The poor people, the working-class people, the people in our neighborhood, they were used to scraping by. It was guys like this."

Dad swept his hand toward the looming mansion.

"For them it was more about losing face than losing money. They couldn't show up at the club anymore. They got cut off from the parties. They worried about what people would say. Their whole importance was tied up in money. There should be no shame in going broke. The dishonor comes from getting rich . . . if you do it the wrong way, if you take advantage of other people."

"Yeah, but people revere wealth," Mom piped in. "They see Donald Trump and they go bananas."

"I cannot, for the life of me, figure that guy out," groused my father. "The Donald is beyond my level of comprehension."

"But he's a star," argued Mom.

"In whose eyes?" Dad shot back.

Then his mood quickly changed and he chuckled to himself. "There were always people staying at our house," he went on. "Johnny Smith, my uncle, lived there on and off for years. Everybody loved Johnny. My father would say, 'Johnny, can ya give us a bit of the "Minstrel Boy"?' and Johnny would get the fiddle from his room and we'd have a night of music. Johnny's flaw was that he liked the bottle and would go on a bit of a bender every now and then but he wasn't mean, although if any pushing or shoving started in a bar, it stopped fast when Johnny stood up. My dad got him a job at the phone company and they'd send Johnny up on the tallest poles. He wasn't afraid of anything. He eventually became a gravedigger. Never married. You would have loved him, Mike."

"And your mom didn't mind having him live in your house off and on for years?" I questioned.

"She encouraged it. She left a room open at the back of the house for people who might need a place to stay. One morning I was eating breakfast and my mom said, 'Tommy, there's a strange man in the back bedroom.' And my dad answered, 'Well, when he wakes up, ask him who he is.' "

"Who was he?" Kerry laughed.

"Hahn," my dad answered. "His last name was Hahn, a Canadian. He was working with Johnny Smith up in Middletown, New York, and got laid off. He had no place to go, so Johnny put him on a train to Paterson and gave him directions to our house along with instructions on how to find the back stairs and where the room with the open bed was. The train arrived late at night and Hahn did what Johnny told him to do."

Matt shook his head. "So, after he woke up, how long did he stay?"

"Three years. He got married out of our house. A few years later a truck pulled up to our front door. It was a bunch of new living-room furniture . . . a gift from Hahn."

My father loved it when people showed their gratitude in humble, genuine ways—Johnny Smith quietly planting tomatoes in their backyard, Hahn sending furniture for their house.

"My mother was a great matchmaker," he continued. " 'Ownie,' she'd say to another visitor, 'I've got a wonderful girl for you.' And the word would go out, and soon Ownie would have a girlfriend. My dad had a joke. 'There's three means of communication,' he'd say, 'telegraph, telephone, and tell-a-woman.' "

Everybody laughed at the corniness of the line, which inspired my father to dig up another funny moment from his childhood.

"There was this lady who used to come over to the house, Clara Delaney. She wasn't totally deaf, but close to it. My mom would shout to her, 'Have ya had somethin' to eat, Clara? Would ya like to join us for dinner?' My mother sort of took to people who had some kind of problem; it could be physical or financial or sometimes loneliness. Well, Clara didn't just have a hearing problem . . ."

My mother interrupted him with her giggling, a certain cue that the story was headed in a southerly direction.

"Her other problem was gas," he said.

My mother's giggle suddenly turned into a high-pitched laugh. Eighty-two years on this earth and the subject of gas still bowls her over. It's amazing, actually.

"Anyway, Clara was always letting them rip," Dad continued over Mom's cackling, "and since she couldn't hear it, she assumed we couldn't either. As my father used to say, 'Clara's so deaf she can't hear herself fart.' Marge says that to me now that I'm having trouble with the ears."

My mother started gasping for air. If you didn't know her, you'd be dialing 911.

"So Clara would be sitting with us at the dining-room table tooting away. One of us might say . . . out loud because she couldn't hear us . . . 'Oh, that was a big one, watch the roof.' And then we'd all laugh. Clara just smiled, thinking someone had told a joke. Then she'd fart again. Oh God, we would laugh, even my mother."

It was a ludicrous scene. With one of the world's great symbols of cultural refinement as a backdrop, its gigantic presence a lasting reminder of good breeding, there we sat, the Leonard clan, three generations of goofballs, yucking it up over a woman who couldn't hear herself fart.

"Oh God," Mom moaned as she finally brought herself under control, "and all I wanted in life was to be classy, like Jackie O."

When Elizabeth returned, she motioned me aside and asked if we would like to spend a night in really comfortable hotel beds. The Inn on Biltmore Estate, a four-star facility, was just a few minutes away. I cautioned her about damaging the Inn's fine reputation by allowing two RVs to pull up to the front and then unload a group of ratty-looking people carrying plastic garbage bags full of clothes, two guitars, and a banjo. Elizabeth laughed and said that it would be an honor for the Biltmore to have us as guests.

"Nice, nice woman," Dad said as we were ushered

into the elegant dining room. The dress code prohibited the wearing of jeans but that's all we had, so the rule was waived and the host sat us at a big table in a far corner.

"Yeah, Elizabeth is cool," I replied. "She told me that she learned a lot from talking with you and this is her thanks."

"She was a good tour guide too," Mom said. "She told me that George Vanderbilt died young, in his fifties, from appendicitis, I think. All that money couldn't save him."

"You can't take it with you," Dad added. "We all leave with nothing."

"But he sure did leave something behind," I said. "That house is some footprint."

"Unbelievable," Matt muttered. "And all that for a family of three. I bet his tombstone is the size of my garage."

"Are your parents buried in Paterson?" Margarita asked my father.

"Yeah, or someplace nearby. I haven't been back since my father died. God, that was back in the late 'sixties. I think the cemetery is actually in Totowa, right next to Paterson. As I remember, it's just a regular gravestone, not very big, with their names on it and the names of my brother and sister."

"What about your parents, Moose?" asked Brendan. "Are they in the same graveyard?"

"My mother is buried in Arizona because she died

when we lived there in the 'seventies. My father . . . yeah, I guess he's . . . I'm not sure. We're not going back to Paterson, are we? There's nothing to see. I heard the place is horrible now."

"Marge, I want to go back," argued my father.

"Why would you want to go back?" she asked. "It's all torn apart. It's gone to hell."

"I want to see the neighborhood, the armory, the firehouse," he pleaded. "I want to remember all the good times we had."

"I saw it once," Mom responded flatly. "I don't need to see it again. Besides, you shouldn't go back in life. It makes you depressed. You should go forward."

Dad didn't seem to hear her last remark. "Fourteen Pennington Street . . . ," he said, almost to himself. "God, they worked so hard to make that place nice for us. All the struggles . . . and they just kept going. Not until I became a parent myself did I realize how they suffered when Tommy and Anna died. But my older sister and I didn't really know that. They kept it from us. Imagine . . . five years old and two. Diphtheria and scarlet fever, things they can fix now. I remember Anna in that little pink dress. And me helping her learn to ride the tricycle. Then she got sick. It didn't take long. Her bed was in the other room. I was in mine and I knew something bad was happening. Then I heard my mother call to my father, 'Tom, our baby is dead.' "

Dad stopped to take a drink of water. Everybody at the table was quiet.

Then he continued. "I peeked out the door of my room. My father had his head on the table. He was crying."

So was my father, eighty-some years later.

My mother shook her head sadly.

"We shouldn't go back."

Eleven

We were supposed to leave the hotel by nine in the morning. That was the plan. It didn't work. It never does. Now I'm starting to sound like my mother.

"But there wasn't any orange juice."

"What's wrong with water?"

I had just opened the Holiday Rambler's front door, and those were the first words I heard as my mother and father started their slow and torturous ascent up the northeast ridge of Mount Everest, also known as the two small retractable metal steps leading into the RV.

"Jesus, if I fall and break my other shoulder . . ."

"Marge, you're not going to fall . . . but I might die of old age if you don't hurry the hell up."

"Hey, you don't want to be feeding me again," she warned.

"At least you'd be getting your orange juice," he countered.

"Oh, big deal," Mom muttered as she took her seat on the RV couch, my father settling in next to her.

"What are you guys arguing about now?" I asked.

"Nothing," Mom answered with a dismissive wave of her hand. "He's just bent out of shape because I took my pills with champagne this morning. When we went back to the room last night there was a nice note from the hotel and a bottle of champagne. I love champagne. It would be a sin to waste it. So I had some this morning to swallow down all the damn pills I have to take."

My father shook his head while I prepared the driver's seat for a productive morning of multitasking—clearing space on the console for my cell phone, my banjo-practice belt, my finger picks, my music CDs, and my can of Red Bull. Through the front windshield, the Winnebago was visible in the far corner of the hotel parking lot. Matt and Margarita were loading in the last of the bulging plastic garbage bags while Brendan and Kerry stood off to one side. They appeared to be arguing. Again.

I settled into the driver's seat and picked up my cell phone. Elizabeth deserved one last expression of gratitude for treating us to the elegant Inn on Biltmore Estate. Even though we looked like rubes—Dad in his new cowboy hat, Mom in her old, makeup-stained tennis cap, our blue jeans, our garbage bags full of clothes, my banjo, and other assorted odds and ends—we seemed to have left the hotel staff with a favorable impression.

"Jack, I can't believe you shit in the bed."

"Me either, that's a first."

Ever have a moment in your life that deserves a one-second soundtrack of that shrill violin from the movie **Psycho**? That was my moment. Caught in a freeze frame, my left hand clutching the cell phone, my right index finger locked an inch above the send button, I stared straight ahead as my heart pounded. The voices were coming from the RV couch, behind me and to the right, and they were much too composed and easygoing considering the subject matter.

"Maybe it was the dessert, but I don't know," Dad said in a nonchalant manner. "I sure wouldn't want to make a habit out of shitting in beds."

I wheeled around. The sudden movement seemed to startle my parents.

"Did I hear right?" I barked. "Are you talking about what I think you're talking about?"

"You mean about your father shitting in the bed?" Mom asked in a matter-of-fact manner.

"Ahhhh . . ." was my only response.

"Yeah," she continued. "Something woke me up at three in the morning, this funny sound." My mother then began rubbing the couch in short, quick strokes to mimic the effect. "Your dad was leaning over the bed with a washcloth or something and was scrubbing the sheets."

Dad looked at me with a sheepish smile as my mother continued with the horror story.

"I said, 'Jack, what the hell are you doing?' And he says, 'Oh, I shit in the bed. But I got it all out.' "

My head felt too light for my body.

"This is unreal," I stammered. "Elizabeth was nice enough to provide each of you with a big, comfy bed and . . ."

"I know," Dad cut me off. "And I shit in it."

Matt had just caught the last line of conversation as he bounded up the RV steps. It stopped him in his tracks.

"Wait," he asked in a befuddled voice. "What did you just say?"

"Good morning Matt," my father replied cheerfully. "I was just telling your dad that I shit in the bed last night. I cleaned it. No big deal. That was nice of Elizabeth, wasn't it? I should have left a thank-you note or something."

Matt's head swiveled hard in my direction. His mouth was slightly open. We stared at each other in baffled silence while my parents resumed their discussion of orange juice versus champagne as a suitable method of pill delivery.

I lay the phone down and started the engine. The call to Elizabeth was put off to a later date. She would have detected the troubling vibrations rattling the shoddy, low-gauge framework of my moral character. I would have told another lie, pretending that everything was perfect, when in fact the Leonards were skedaddling out of state after shitting in the hand that bed us.

As we drove away from the Biltmore, Matt surreptitiously dialed his cell phone and whispered the awful news to Margarita, Kerry, and Brendan, who were following in the Winnebago. I could hear muffled screams coming from the earpiece. Once the initial shock wore off, however, a curious emotion lingered.

Admiration.

A crude indignity of old age had been casually swatted away like a bothersome gnat. Instead of being pummeled into depression by the one physical failing few choose to talk about, my mother and father had instead made light of it. The mortifying moment had been devalued.

This was not a new strategy. My parents have never had a problem exposing their flaws and laughing at their mistakes. They were human, and all humans have failings. Growing up in that kind of environment gave me strength. I didn't have to be perfect or pretend to be smarter or more accomplished than I was. By openly acknowledging many of my own weaknesses and fears—math, roller coasters, bugs, muddy-bottomed lakes, etcetera—I had taken most of the ammunition away from the people who might have wanted to make fun of me. I could try and fail and try and fail again without worry of ridicule. Years later, after trying and failing more times than I would have liked, it finally paid off.

From Asheville we traveled northeast, stopping for the night in a campground near Winston-Salem, North Carolina, before continuing on through Greensboro, Burlington, and Durham on our way to the Virginia border. The plan was to camp somewhere in Virginia and then head for northern Maryland to visit the small school where my father went to college. Noticing on the map that the route took us through Richmond, I grabbed the cell phone and called Don and Julien in the hopes of spicing up what would have been just a boring travel day.

Don Jones and Julien Scott, Richmond natives, had come into our lives during a taping of **The Brendan Leonard Show.** The episode was shot at Disney World in Orlando, Florida, where a segment was built around a spur-of-the-moment contest to see which of Brendan's friends could emerge from one of the park's souvenir shops dressed in the dorkiest Disneyesque tourist attire. Don and Julien, walking by with a group of fellow African-Americans, made some amusing, off-the-cuff comments and we pressed them into service as judges of the contest. They were funny, creative guys, and their phone numbers were jotted in my book for future reference.

I reached Don first and explained the particulars, hoping that he and Julien could take my concept of touring the country with a couple of elderly people and give it a new spin. Their spin involved plopping my eighty-seven-year-old father into the driver's seat of a souped-up go-cart, then challenging him to a race. It sounded like a great idea. Dad had just been stripped of his driver's license. Maybe this would make him feel young again. To that end, Don, a stocky guy in his early thirties, and Julien, in his mid-twenties, his hair in cornrows and a scary tattoo on his neck, were encouraged to treat my father as if he were one of their running mates, which they happily did.

Gentlemen, start your trash talking.

"I don't know what to do right now," threatened Julien as he paced in front of my father. "I'm contemplating whether to take it easy or bring my 'A' game."

Don picked it up from there. "No mercy," he hissed.

"Yeah," nodded Julien. "Mercy's for the weak."

My father answered with a smile. Given the noise from the other engines, his tight-fitting racing helmet, his bad ear, and the fact that two street-schooled black guys were jamming his language radar with a rapid-fire verbal style not often used on the Golf Channel, my father was totally missing the point of what I was trying to accomplish. He looked at me, blinked, and gave a weak thumbs-up signal.

"Why did we come here?" moaned my mother. "I'm a wreck."

My father wasn't. He didn't have time, driving off the go-cart course and into the pits after just one lap. So much for the idea of opening up the throttle to make him feel young again.

"No more of that stuff," announced my mother as I steered the RV out of the go-cart parking lot and toward the highway to Williamsburg, our destination for the evening. Dad was sitting on the wooden folding chair, its feet rattling with every small bump on the highway.

"Never did like speed," he said with a smile. "But nice, nice people. Excellent. I really enjoyed talking with your friends. Wonderful fellows . . . interesting guys."

"I saw them talking to you after the race," I said. "What were they saying?"

Dad answered with a smile. "I haven't got a clue."

We arrived in the historic town of Williamsburg just before darkness but the shops were closed, so we had dinner at a restaurant and headed for the campsite and our beds. The next morning long icicles were hanging from the Holiday Rambler's side mirrors, a reminder that we were back in cold country. My fa-

Go-cart team "talking tough" prior
to one-lap flame-out. Brendan, Don
Jones, Jack, and Julien Scott.

ther, however, was doing his best to warm things up,
having disappeared from the RV to chat with the
campground maintenance staff. When it was time to
leave, he couldn't be found.

"Tweeeeeet. Tweeeeeeeeeeeet."

My mom is one of the few women I know who
can purse her lips and blast out a shrill, ear-piercing
whistle. That's how she used to call us in from the
park when we were kids.

"Hell, he can't hear anyway," she muttered, leaning back in from the Holiday Rambler's open front

door. "This ticks me off. If he were a girl, he'd be pregnant all the time. He can't say no to anybody."

"Or good-bye," I added. "It'll look like the conversation's over . . . he walks two or three steps away, then turns around and goes back."

"The curtain call." She nodded. "Rev the engine. Hell with it, just leave . . . Oh wait, here he comes . . . and he's only got a sweater on! What the hell's wrong with him?"

My father climbed into the RV. A look of guilt was plastered all over his cold, red face.

"Where were you?" my mother demanded.

"I was talking to the man, thanking him. He was so nice."

"But Jack, you've got just a sweater on."

"Warm heart, Marge." My father tapped his chest with an index finger. "Jeez," he continued. "The people have been so good. You have to say good-bye to them."

"You said good-bye earlier," my mother argued.

"Well, I said good-bye again," he countered. "It never hurts. He can erase it."

Mom sat down on the couch and shook her head. "You'll probably call him up when you get home," she sighed.

"Maybe," Dad said, smiling. "I got his number."

"God help him," she said.

"Marge, your mother would have said good-bye to him."

"Not ten times," she shot back.

Dad plopped down in the easy chair, took off his hat, and scratched the top of his head.

"Well," he sighed. "You can't win 'em all, Mike."

From Williamsburg we headed north through Fredericksburg, Alexandria, and Washington, D.C., before crossing into Maryland. All in all, the driving was easy and the traffic relatively light.

**"Oh the night that Mary died, she called me
     to her side
     and willed to me her old, red BVDs . . ."**

I don't think it was the state of Maryland that jarred another song out of my father's vault of strange tunes; it was his state of mind. We were headed for his alma mater, Mount Saint Mary's College in Emmitsburg, and he was flying high. Dad continued singing.

"I learned that one in college," he announced. "Oh jeez, Mike, you're gonna love this place."

Mount Saint Mary's is a small, well-respected Catholic college on a hilly patch of land in northern Maryland. My father had never heard of the school until a month before classes started. He had graduated from Paterson's Saint Joseph's High School and was serving Mass for a visiting priest who asked about his plans. My dad told him that he was hoping to get into nearby Seton Hall University but hadn't yet heard from the admissions department.

Young Jack at Mount Saint Mary's University in
Emmitsburg, Maryland.

The priest suggested Mount Saint Mary's, having had some kind of connection. An application form was filled out, and a few weeks later my dad was straddling a steamer trunk in the open back rumble seat of a small car driven by two buddies headed for someplace beyond Maryland. It was 11:00 P.M. when they dropped him off at a random building on the campus.

"I rang the bell," my father recounted. "And Father McCormick opened the door. 'Balls' McCormick, we called him."

I didn't ask why.

"Balls took one look at me," Dad continued, "and said, 'Boy, are you dusty.' From then on everyone at Mount Saint Mary's knew me as 'Dusty.' I hated that name. That was one good thing about getting out of there in four years. Nobody called me 'Dusty' again."

Dad was keyed up. Nearly a half century had passed since his last visit. He had spent a good part of the morning picking out his clothes, trying on one clean shirt, then another and another. The two RVs were parked side by side in a lot behind a rural Maryland restaurant, about an hour from Emmitsburg. We had ordered take-out food and were gathered inside the Holiday Rambler, listening to my father talk in excited tones about how special a college education was in the midst of the Depression. Only two or three students from his high school graduating class had had the wherewithal to continue their studies.

He got the chance because of the money his mother had been putting away, bit by bit, through the years. A college diploma was a big deal to a woman who never finished grammar school.

"The total bill was under a thousand dollars," Dad said between bites of his sandwich, careful not to spill anything on his clean shirt. "And that was everything—tuition, room and board, everything. My father saw the campus once. It was my graduation."

"What about your mom?" asked Margarita.

"No, she never saw it," he replied quietly, pausing to take a sip from his bottled water.

"I came home for Christmas break during my second year," Dad continued. "We drove to New York City to meet a friend of the family, Mae Kramer, and to see the Christmas lights. New York is only thirteen miles from Paterson, so it's an easy trip. It was my mother, my father, my older sister Mary, and myself. We parked the car and were walking down the sidewalk when my mom fell to the ground. I didn't know what happened. My dad was on his knees trying to help her but she wasn't moving. Mae fumbled through her purse, found a little book, and opened it to a page. She gave it to me and told me to start reading. It was prayers for the dying. But my mother was already dead."

The RV was quiet. I had known that my father was a young man when his mother died, but the details had been missing. Now he was filling them in:

the Christmas lights, the prayer book, Mae Kramer, and more.

"My father was really broken up. It was an aneurism, we later learned. She had gone to the doctor earlier in the day, but never told us. A hearse came and took her to the New York City Morgue. We got home about midnight. The next morning I didn't know what to do, I was just nineteen, so I walked around Paterson and went into a store, Gray's Haberdashery. Leschie Breslin worked there. She knew our family. I said I needed to buy a black tie. She asked me why a black one and I said it was for a funeral. Whose funeral, she wanted to know. My mother's, I said. Mrs. Breslin burst into tears."

"Was it a big funeral?" I asked.

"Saint Joseph's was packed," Dad replied. "My mother had been so nice to people. They all came out. But we didn't have the funeral right away. There was a delay because we couldn't get her body out of New York City. We sent Charlie Scanlon, the undertaker, to bring her back home, but there was all this red tape because she died out of state. They had to make sure there wasn't foul play, that we didn't kill her. It was hard on my father. He just wanted her to be home and not in that morgue all alone. We finally got her back and had the wake in the house. It was two days. Johnny Smith never left her side, sat in a chair by the coffin the whole time, didn't sleep for two nights. Then we buried her and after Christmas I went back to school."

As my father took another sip from his bottle of water I glanced over at Brendan. He would have been a college sophomore had he not dropped out for a semester to join us on the journey. Like my father, Brendan is easygoing and caring. He loves music and is good at sports. His high school coaches, however, were always a bit disappointed that he didn't use his six-foot-four-inch frame to punish opponents. The reasons were genetic. Like my father, Brendan hates to see people get hurt.

"Are you getting the jitters?" I yelled back to my father as we rolled past the first highway sign for Emmitsburg.

"No jitters," he called out. "Just happiness thinking of all the great times."

"But that was before you started going out with me," Mom wisecracked from across the RV aisle.

"I know," Dad replied. "And you brought a ray of sunshine."

"And thunder," she mumbled.

Dad chuckled. "Thunder is right," he said in a stage whisper.

It was a cold but clear mid-February day. The rolling hills were dotted with patches of snow.

"Will there be anybody there who knows you?" asked Matt from the passenger seat.

"I think there's one priest left," my father responded. "He was a year ahead of me in college, then he went into the seminary. His name is Father Fives.

I'm hoping and praying that he's there. He'll remember me. I hope . . . Look ahead, Marge, Roddy's Creek. Roddy used to live on the foot of the campus. Oh jeez, we're getting close."

It was early afternoon when we drove onto the hilly Mount Saint Mary's campus and parked behind a gymnasium. We hadn't called the college to arrange for any special treatment because . . . well, we didn't want any special treatment. Dad wasn't a big-shot alumnus or a heavy donor, so there was no expectation of a red-carpet welcome. He just wanted to show off the pretty campus, say hello to Father Fives, and get a campus official to back his claims of how special "The Mount" was.

"It's gorgeous, isn't it?" Dad exclaimed as he led us up a sidewalk and toward a collection of older-looking buildings. "See that window on the left, second floor? That was my room . . . me and Johnny Backus." My father chuckled to himself. "Johnny's father came to see him once and slipped a ten-dollar bill into one of his schoolbooks. He came back the next time . . . the ten dollars was still there. And Johnny was telling his father how hard he studied."

Dad laughed again. On the pathway ahead there was a water fountain.

"Every student, when I was here, took a drink of water on the way to class." My dad bent over and took a swig. "Ahhh," he nodded. "Still good."

After asking around we were directed to the campus bookstore. My father led the way. It was difficult to keep up with his pace.

"This is his Super Bowl," Margarita commented to me as we entered the bookstore. "This is the best part of the trip for him, wouldn't you say?"

"Yeah," I nodded. "And wait until he corrals somebody from the college. We'll never get out of here."

As my mother looked over a collection of Mount Saint Mary's coffee mugs, my dad found a bookstore employee who gave him access to a telephone and Father Fives's number. I walked over to eavesdrop on the conversation.

"Do you remember me?" my dad asked excitedly. "Do ya . . . a year behind you . . . yeah . . . you were our example . . . we all wanted to be as smart as you . . . remember Father McCormick's poem?

" '. . . if you haven't got the necessary credits,
you can't expect to graduate from
here . . . and you'll never have the necessary
credits, if you're always down at Fritz's
drinking beer.' "

Dad laughed, then explained why he was in the area and asked if it was possible to meet somewhere on campus for a few minutes. There was a long pause while he listened, his smile gradually fading away.

"You do?" he asked quietly. "Of what . . . oh. I

went through it, prostate and stuff. I took sixty-four treatments . . . Oh . . . Oh jeez . . . Well, you've had a good life . . . you know, we have a lot to thank God for . . . Yeah . . . Yeah . . . We'll be praying for you . . . You were the smartest one in school . . . Thank you for talking with me. I hope you feel better . . . Bye-bye."

My father gave the phone back to the store clerk, thanked her for making the call, then walked slowly over to my mother.

"Father Fives is dying of cancer," he said.

"So you won't be able to see him?" my mother asked.

"No," Dad replied softly. "He's too sick to get up."

A few moments of silence followed. My father seemed disoriented, scratching his head, then shuffling a few steps away from us, then back, then away again, lost in thought. He had envisioned a glorious homecoming, a backslapping welcome from someone who remembered the skinny Irish kid from Paterson . . . the baseball player . . . the good-time Charlie . . . the guy who would do anything for anybody.

"Let's go to the administration office," he finally said with a look of renewed enthusiasm. "They'll be excited to know that we came all this way to pay a visit. I think there's only a few from my class who are still alive."

We followed my father up one hallway and down the next, watching as he cheerfully poked his head into rooms along the way to announce his presence and to ask where he might find a college official who could spare five minutes for an old alum. He was finally directed to a reception area guarded by a middle-aged woman sitting behind a big counter. Dad introduced himself and asked if he could say a quick hello to whomever it was that occupied the office behind her.

"He is not in right now," she said. "He's in meetings all afternoon until after four."

"On the campus?" my dad asked.

"On the campus," she replied.

"Why don't we break him out of one?" he said with a chuckle, then introduced her to my mom and Matt, who was carrying a small movie camera. Matt asked the woman for permission to videotape the exchange, explaining that we might eventually make a story out of the trip to air on the **Today** show. She agreed to let Matt roll the camera, and while I was outside making phone calls my father made yet another request for a moment with the campus official.

"He's in a faculty meeting until after four P.M.," the woman repeated.

"I'd like to really . . . we've come four thousand miles . . . ," Dad stammered.

"Well, what can you do, Jack?" interrupted Mom with a touch of sarcasm. "They didn't know you were coming."

"Well, is there anyone here that I could talk to?" Dad asked meekly.

"Let's see," the woman replied, looking at some kind of list. "Who would you know?"

"I don't know anybody," said my father. "I'm an old man."

The receptionist then began calling out names from the list. She didn't get it. Or maybe she was being evasive. Dad continued his friendly banter, smiling and laughing to no avail.

"Well, I'd like to see somebody as long as I've come this far," he said, a sad and defeated look creeping onto his face. The only response from the woman was to ask whom he might know.

At this point I would have lost my patience. She was going by the book, thinking small. We didn't have an appointment. And that was that. The old man had traveled from across the country in an RV. He had his wife, his son, three grandchildren, and a grandchild's wife with him. On top of that, there was a good chance that six million **Today** show viewers would watch at least a part of his college homecoming.

"I don't know who else to refer you to," she said. "Do you ever come up for the reunions?"

"No," Dad replied in exasperation. "I haven't been back but once since I graduated." Then he tried again, in a friendly voice, to explain how we had been on the road for almost three weeks and that a visit to Mount Saint Mary's was seen as a highlight of a tour that was to include stops in his birthplace and the naval base where he served during the war.

"I'm sorry," she repeated. "I don't know who to refer you to."

If I had been in the room at the time I would have gotten angry. Forget all that crap about not knowing whom to refer him to. There were no classes that day, but plenty of people were around. Grab a student, a maintenance worker, anybody! Give the old man ten minutes. Show him the new cafeteria. Hand him a catalog. Welcome him back, for God's sake. How hard could that be?

"Well, thank you very much."

That's all the anger my father could muster as he walked slowly out of the office and off the campus with his head bowed. Only later, after looking at Matt's videotape of the conversation, did I know its details, and by then it was too late. We were settled in at the Yogi Bear Campground in Williamsport, Maryland. Dad had gone outside to take a walk.

"That's why I don't like to go back in life," Mom said as she sipped wine from a paper cup. "You have these high expectations about what it's going to be like and it never is. Then you get sad. That part of your life is over. Leave it and move on."

"But I wouldn't have let that woman dictate the events," I said. "I'm sure people from the college would have welcomed him with open arms had they known what was going on. You just have to bypass the people who get in the way."

"Yeah, but you know your father," she sighed.

"He's nice to everybody. I would have told her to stick it."

"Me too."

That hasn't always been my style. During the early part of my life, I was reluctant to stand up for anything. Shyness, fear, stupidity—take your pick—all of those factors kept me from defending any worthwhile position. When people were being picked on, I stayed silent. When moral causes needed leadership, I vanished from sight. Fitting in seemed more important than standing out. In some respects, it still does. Not that my kids would know.

They think I'm Mr. Tough Guy. I work out hard. I'm strong for my age. I did some boxing at a ghetto gym as a forty-year-old. When people are rude, I almost always say something. Is that courage or foolishness? Mostly the latter, I'm guessing. As for the reason behind my late-onset development of thinner skin . . . I point the finger at parenthood. Protecting the nest, so to speak.

One of the early episodes happened when Matt was about eleven. He was a coordinated little boy, but too laid-back and carefree for big-time competitive sports. He enjoyed playing because he enjoyed playing, even if it meant not winning. Still, like most of his classmates, he signed up for kid's baseball and was put on a team with a meathead coach. I'm not calling him a meathead because my son rode the bench. Matt didn't care and since he didn't care, I didn't. We'd drop him off at the ballpark, he'd sit on the bench, play maybe an inning, and then come home as happy as he'd left.

Near the end of the season a conflict arose. Cathy's younger sister Joan was getting married and asked Matt if he could be an altar server at the wedding, scheduled on a game day. I told Matt to call the coach and let him know—not that a benchwarmer would be missed, but it was the right thing to do. A few minutes later Matt came back to the room with a puzzled look. He said that the coach had yelled at him, saying he was a loser for abandoning the team. I had always preached against the practice of parents butting in with coaches and teachers. Children needed to train for the inevitable coming of a lunatic boss. Why rob them of that rehearsal time?

This, however, was a special case. The lunatic had arrived early. So I called him.

"Hi. This is Mike Leonard," I began. "My son Matt just called you to say that he couldn't make the . . . Hello . . . Hello . . ."

The lunatic had hung up on me. I dialed again. Somebody else answered the phone. From the sound of his voice, I guessed that he was in his late teens.

"Hi," I said. "Can I talk to your dad?"

"He's not home," the kid replied.

"Yeah, he is," I shot back. "I talked to him less than thirty seconds ago."

"He's not here."

"All right. Let me leave a message, then." My voice was calm. "Please tell your father that he's a piece of shit. From the looks of him he's never played an inning of anything and if he had any guts he'd come over here so I could kick his fat ass for hanging up on me. And by the way, you're a shithead too for telling me he's not there when you know and I know he is. You got that, scumbag? . . . Hello . . . Hello . . ."

The lunatic's son had hung up on me. I put the phone into its cradle and turned around to see Matt standing there with a quizzical look on his sweet face. I hadn't known that he was still in the room. What could I say? A smarter man would have figured out a better way to handle the situation with Mr. Meathead and Son of Meathead. The same can be said for my encounter, a year later, with a car full of hot-rodding teenage punks. Yes, the guy behind the wheel was acting irresponsibly by laying rubber in the grammar-school parking lot where Megan's scout troop was playing, but a more mature person wouldn't have pulled the driver out of the car by his neck, as I did, then threatened to punch his lights out in front of a dozen mesmerized Brownies. More encounters followed: the spirited pursuit of the surly litterbug, the rude librarian's much-needed reprimand, the dressing down of the haughty airline passenger, and on and on. Were they legitimate battles or self-gratifying displays of false courage? Let the shrinks decide.

"Happy birthday, Cath."

"Thanks, Mick. How are you holding up?"

I had stepped outside a restaurant in Williamsport to call my wife. True to form, she was more concerned about my feelings than taking a bow on her special day.

"Oh, I'm fine. But something happened earlier that pissed me off."

I told her what had happened at the college, how the woman failed to grasp the significance of the situation and how my father didn't do anything to fight his way past the human roadblock.

"How did Moose react?"

"Just the way you'd expect. She let some swear words fly, but not until we got back in the RV. She knows the score. My dad hates conflict. It's amazing the two of them have managed to stay together for sixty years, seeing how different they are. But somehow at the end of the day they always seem to iron things out."

The conversation shifted to how much we missed each other, then to the latest news on each child. Megan's last ultrasound was coming up and even though the baby hadn't been kicking much, there were no indications that he or she would arrive early. Cathy and I said good night to each other with a reminder of how different our lives would be in a matter of days or weeks.

"West Woods . . . Union General John Sedgwick lost more than twenty-two hundred men in less than a half hour in an ill-fated charge into these woods against Jackson's troops."

It was the next morning, and Brendan was sitting in the Holiday Rambler reading aloud from the visitor's guide to Antietam as we slowly drove through the perfectly preserved Civil War battlefield just outside Sharpsburg, Maryland. There were no other vehicles in the state park, which allowed us to creep along the narrow paved road that curved through the immense field, so quiet and peaceful now.

"It's eerie, isn't it?" I said to no one in particular. "It looks just like the old photos in the Civil War books. They've kept it the same, the little stone bridge, the cannons, the wood fences . . . The only thing missing is the fighting."

"Boy, can you imagine the thoughts in their minds?" Dad added, his wounded feelings from yesterday's college visit mostly healed. "Knowing they're going to be five feet away and it's either you or him."

In one day, over twenty thousand soldiers were killed or wounded at Antietam. The tranquil, rolling farmland was dotted with statues and stone monuments memorializing those with the will to fight.

To the Georgia Confederates:

We sleep here in obedience to law; When duty called, we came, when country called, we died.

To the Union soldiers from New Jersey:

You have sustained the reputation of your state and done credit to your officers and yourselves. While we lament the death of our brave comrades who have fallen so gloriously we can only commend their souls to God and their sorrowing friend to his sure protection.

"I don't know why people can't settle their differences at a bargaining table," Dad said. "Killing people never makes anything better."

"But what are you going to do?" Mom responded. "There are bad people in the world. You can't just let them have their way. Sometimes you have to fight."

Dad stayed silent as we slowly drove through a peaceful cornfield where thousands had died.

Twelve

"Man, everything about this place is weird."

Brendan had just bounded into the Holiday Rambler to join the rest of us for an early breakfast.

"I was afraid to leave the Winnebago because these two strange dogs showed up. A white bulldog and the fattest wiener dog I've ever seen. You can't see its legs. It looks like a hovercraft."

Kerry jumped out of her seat to peer through the front windshield.

"Where are they . . . Oh, my God! It looks like a seal."

I hustled to the window, followed by Matt and Margarita. My parents remained seated at the dinette table, having just poured milk into their white Styrofoam cereal bowls.

"Look at those legs!" Margarita gasped.

"They're like cigar butts," marveled Matt. "Are we on top of some kind of nuclear waste dump? The people are mutants and so are the pets."

We had crossed the border into western New Jersey the night before, and for the first time since the journey began our campsite options were limited. All the accredited places listed in our guidebook were closed for the season, leaving us to choose between a Wal-Mart parking lot and an unrated campground that supposedly had hookups for water and electricity. The decision was made to roll the dice and head for the campground, realizing only seconds after stepping out of the vehicles that we had crapped out in a big way.

"I think I just stepped in dog crap," Kerry moaned, shining a flashlight at her feet. "Jeez, it's all over the place. What a dump!"

Carved into the side of a wooded hill, the darkened, trash-strewn campground was home to a haphazard collection of run-down RVs, a few of them occupied by people who had apparently cut the knot with society, choosing instead to live out the rest of their disillusioned days in Camp Dog Doo. All kinds of wires, some dangling from poles and trees, some crisscrossing the ground, most, I would guess, spliced and patched from a pirated source, gave the place an added look of danger. That's another fear of mine, electricity, born from the shocking experience of getting shocked while working one summer as a janitor in a Chicago high-rise apartment complex. I was using wet steel wool to scrub some decorative tile above a kitchen counter and should have known to steer clear of the electrical outlet. I didn't. The resulting shower of sparks and Jerry Lee Lewis–like leg-twitching spasm left me distrustful of anything voltage-related. Don't ask me to jump your car. I will not do it.

While shining our flashlights at the surrounding mess, a bearded, shirtless man with a big belly emerged from the RV closest to us. My first inclination was to ask why he wasn't wearing a shirt in the middle of winter, but something told me to skip that question. Instead, I called out a friendly hello. He answered with a stare. That usually sets off an alarm on my internal rudeness detector, prompting me to call out a rhetorical answer to my own greeting. "Hi there," I'd call out to myself. This time, however, I held my tongue, preferring silence to a hail of bullets.

We made it through the night without being murdered, and now the five of us were staring through the RV window at Camp Doo's rendition of pets on parade.

"Seal Dog and Gerry Cooney!" I exclaimed.

Brendan gave me a quizzical look. "Why Gerry Cooney?"

"Because he's a white boxer," I replied.

"But it's a bulldog," said Brendan.

"It is?" I looked back out at the two dogs waddling

through a minefield of their own droppings. "Bull-dog . . . boxer . . . whatever . . . how would I know?"

"Didn't you say you had a dog when you were a kid?" Brendan asked.

"We did. But not for long. Inky went insane."

"Insane?" wondered Matt. "How do you judge the sanity of a dog?"

"Well, it was pretty obvious that Inky was delusional. He had a Rin Tin Tin complex, always acting bigger and tougher than he was. He was a little black mutt living in a . . . what breed was Rin Tin Tin? Who cares . . . one time he went for Timmy's throat, and we . . ."

"Remember our queer cat?" interrupted my mother, derailing the story of Inky's rapid descent into madness. "Jeez, I'd sit in that den chair and it would jump into my lap and try to nurse. And it was a girl cat. It had to be gay."

My mother's giggle triggered gales of laughter from Kerry.

"Then Kevin brought that lizard home from the circus," she continued. "I forgot, what do they call the kind that change colors?"

"Chameleons," I replied, and then explained the situation to the younger members of our traveling party. "Vendors would go around with a box of chameleons. They had little string leashes around their necks with safety pins at one end. It was a craze that never took off, pinning live jewelry to your clothes . . . jewelry that would always match. Put on a yellow shirt, the chameleon turns yellow. Put on a green shirt, the thing turns green."

"Did it work?" asked Margarita.

"We never found out," I answered. "Pogo ate the chameleon."

"Pogo?"

"Pogo was the next-door neighbor's dog," I continued. "A big yellow . . . was it a Lab? I don't know. Anyway, dogs were free to wander in those days and Kevin had tied the chameleon to a wrought-iron railing on the back steps. He wanted to give it a little sun. When Kevin went back out to check on his lizard, he found Pogo sitting on the steps with the safety-pin end of the leash dangling from his mouth. Imagine how bad a lizard would taste!"

My father smiled. "I've had worse," he said with a quick, sideways nod in my mother's direction. She responded with a bored shrug.

"I think a bird takes the cake," said Kerry. "You see those nature shows where a snake kills a bird then swallows it whole . . . feathers, claws, a beak . . . all for about a thimble full of meat. You know when you eat popcorn and that little brown shell thing gets lodged in the back corner of your throat? Try getting a bird claw out."

Seal Dog and Cooney, in the meantime, had shuffled off, perhaps in search of a romantic spot between turd piles to work on a new, horrifying breed. It was now safe to go outside and start the RV decoupling process.

"Be careful where you step," I warned Brendan as he put on his coat. "Just having to say that reminds me of Ricky Leslie's theory—you know, my friend who got clotheslined by the wet paint wire?—he thinks our generation is a lot savvier than your generation because of our early awareness training with dog doo. You always had to keep on the lookout. It taught us be wary."

"Who taught you guys to wear your pants up to your armpits?" Brendan cracked as he stepped down the RV stairs.

The electrical plugs were pulled, the water hoses detached, and off we went, happy to make our escape before the big-bellied, shirtless man awoke. The get-away from Seal Dog and Cooney wasn't quite as clean. I couldn't shake the mental picture of their imagined romantic encounter. That disturbing visual was coupled with a reflection on what their offspring might look like. Jabba the Hut in green boxing shorts came to mind.

We drove due east and then north on our way to Morristown and the College of Saint Elizabeth's, my mother's alma mater. She always spoke highly of the school but wasn't nearly as jacked as my father had been on the way to Mount Saint Mary's. Going backward in life didn't interest her, not that she forgot what was learned along the way. Nothing escapes my mother's mind, as was demonstrated during a brief snack stop along Route 287. She was sitting at the dinette table when the words suddenly came flying out.

"Within the elastic limits, all elastic elongations, bends, and twists are comparable to the forces causing them."

A brief pause followed, and then in a singsong voice she cried out, "Very good!"

"What the hell was that?" I asked.

"Newton's law," Mom replied.

"What does it mean?"

"I have no idea," she answered, shaking her head, then taking a bite from a muffin before continuing. "I was a pretty good student. I could memorize anything."

Marge yawning through the college lecture on the importance of keeping curfew.

"Were you wild?" I asked.

"Sort of . . . one time we disrupted the glee club concert. It was Seton Hall's . . . the men . . . the conductor had to stop the concert and ask the girls in the front row to kindly behave. Somebody would give a hand signal and we would all cross our legs at the same time. All of a sudden a nun comes down with a pencil and paper looking at us and writing our names down. We got two weeks.

"Another time . . . I didn't get campused for this but it was funny . . . There was this girl, she was neat as a pin—you know, one of those real prissy things—everything in her drawers was perfect, and the other girls in our group bet me that I wouldn't rumple up her dresser drawers. And I did. She went out, I snuck in, and . . ."

My mother whirled her arms back and forth, pantomiming the ransacking of a room.

"Oh . . . she threw a fit! And her dad used to drive us home. She said, 'You're not going home this weekend with my father.' And I had to stay there. She didn't talk to me for two weeks. She got over that. She was in my wedding. Her husband's now in a veteran's home with Alzheimer's."

We proceeded north on 287 before exiting onto a winding country road through a beautiful stretch of rolling hills and fine homes. New Jersey gets a bum rap, as do other states and cities, based on clichéd references made by people who need to keep their labels simple, the core of their beliefs solid. My core was cracking, each day of the journey, each mile driven, causing the cracks to widen even more.

If my mom is such a pessimist, I mused, why does she claim to look only toward the future? If my dad's optimism was truly eternal, I wondered, why does he focus so fondly on the past? And what about me? Through the years I had developed what I thought was a sense of toughness by pushing through adversity to make things happen. But now I was asking myself, who's tougher, someone who tries to change the world to suit his style or somebody who stands there and takes everything that life throws at him?

Boom.

"Oh, my God!" Mom cried out. "Did you hit your head?"

My father had fallen. He was on the floor of the RV, the toppled wooden folding chair lying on top of his legs.

The damn wooden folding chair.

He had repeatedly ignored our warnings and now he was down, holding his head, while my mother tried to work her way back to him as the moving RV pitched and rolled through the hilly countryside.

"I'm all right," he mumbled as my mother and Matt tried to help him get up. The two-lane road was narrow, and there was no place to pull off and stop. I felt myself getting angry.

"You knew these roads have a lot of curves," I yelled from the driver's seat. "Why do you keep sitting in that chair?"

"To look at the paper," he responded meekly as Matt guided him to the recliner.

"But you can read the paper from any seat," I argued. "It was like you were asking for it. I mean, what do you think . . ."

"I'm okay . . . okay," he interrupted. "It's over with. No problem."

My anger was mixed with sorrow. An eighty-seven-year-old man doesn't fall lightly. I knew that the tumble had given him a jolt, but it could easily have been avoided. The road ahead was full of dips and curves. It was impossible to see what was beyond the next turn. What if we had to stop suddenly or swerve to avoid an oncoming car? My dad had taken an unnecessary tumble, banged his head in the process, and then struggled back to his feet, hoping that his attempt to act as if nothing happened would brighten our moods. It didn't.

"Jesus, everybody's on my ass," he muttered, mostly to himself.

By late morning we were closing in on Morristown. My father had a slight bruise on his forehead but seemed okay, overriding whatever discomfort he might have been feeling with enthusiastic cheerleading, aimed at my mother.

"Starting to look familiar, eh, Marge? You getting excited?"

"Yep," she answered indifferently while looking out the window. "They don't know I'm coming, so we'll just get a quick look and move on. I'm hungry."

The campus was small and parking was limited but a security guard, upon hearing my brief explanation of the journey, allowed us to leave the RVs on the side of an access road behind what looked like an administration building. We walked in and found our way to the president's office, but were told that she was at a campus seminar that was to be followed by a Mass and then a special luncheon and therefore would be unavailable. My mother nodded pleasantly. The woman in the office noticed our home video cameras and asked if the pictures were for our own viewing. Matt said yes, then mentioned that some of the material might make its way on to the **Today** show as part of a series about the journey. Off we were sent to another office, where a mid-level administrator didn't seem all that interested in the prospect of her tiny college getting a **Today** show PR boost.

So we left.

The lukewarm college reception, in some ways, paralleled what had happened to my father . . . with one big exception. My mother didn't care.

"Well, I saw it," she said as we walked back to the RVs. "Let's move on."

From Morristown we headed toward Paterson, in the northeast tip of the state. As rough as the city had become, I was eager to see where my parents' houses were located—my mother's on Market Street, my father's on Pennington. And what about the armory, the firehouse, and Saint Joseph's church? Would they look the way I had pictured them? Could the sight of present-day storefronts and sidewalks be helpful when conjuring up the storied images of Happy Mahoney serving ice cream or Mr. Cristillo making his weekly rounds?

Tony Cristillo, whose backyard butted up against my mother's, sold insurance for Metropolitan Life. One of his clients was Tom Leonard, and every Thursday afternoon Mr. Cristillo would stop by the Leonard house to collect the weekly premium. It was twenty cents. Tony's son Lou and Tom's son Jack became friendly, tossing the ball around and going to sporting events together. Lou was a good athlete and a tough kid. He was also very funny, quitting high school to join the vaudeville comedy circuit. After a rough early go he found a partner, and the two hit the road together. Lou changed his last name to Costello. The other guy stuck with his real name. It was Abbott.

Years later, my father was working for **Time** magazine and had to go to California for business. The manager of **Time**'s Los Angeles office picked my father up at his hotel and while driving to the appointment asked if my dad knew anybody in the entertainment business. The man's two young daughters were dying of cystic fibrosis, and he was desperate to cheer them up with an autographed picture of somebody famous. My father called Lou Costello, and a few hours later the two little girls were eating hot dogs and laughing it up in the Beverly Hills backyard of one of the biggest comedy stars of all time.

After lunch Lou motioned my father into the house, telling him that someone was waiting on the telephone. It was long distance, a big deal in the mid-1950s. My dad picked up the receiver and said a tentative hello . . . only to hear his father, three thousand miles away, respond in kind. It was Lou's doing, another small gesture of kindness from the Paterson kid who made it big.

"Oh my God!" my father gasped. "It's gone."

We were driving through the heart of Paterson. The city that he remembered had been wiped off the face of the earth.

"Let's get out of here," moaned my mother. "This is scary."

Down the dirty, potholed streets we moved. Slow-motion scenes of a ruined city, framed by the RV windows, played out before my parents' disbelieving eyes. They had known that Paterson had taken a hit, but this was way beyond what they had expected to see. The narrow side streets were lined with parked cars, many of them stripped, burned-out shells. Broken bottles were everywhere. Refuse spilled from tipped-over garbage cans. Newspaper pages and empty plastic shopping bags blew past small groups of people staring sullenly at the odd sight of two huge RVs squeezing through the mess of boarded-up stores and abandoned lots.

"Look at the armory!" my father cried out as we drove into view of a wrecked, shuttered building, its dirty red bricks covered with graffiti. "And the firehouse . . . where did it go?"

"Is that Saint Joe's?" asked my mother in disbelief. "Jesus."

There would be no stopping to light a candle in the church where Annie Smith was eulogized, where my parents were married, and where I was baptized. The scarred front door had been chained shut. "This was the nicest church in Paterson," said my father.

"Was," said my mother.

"Was," he quietly repeated.

We turned a corner and circled back to Pennington Street. A small group of men glared in our direction as we moved past them. One of the men yelled something. Another gave us the finger. My dad leaned his bruised forehead closer to the side window, straining to see what had become of the house that his father had maintained with such care.

"That can't be it," he said, almost in a whisper. "That just can't be it."

The broken-down structure bore no resemblance to what he remembered. The front door was open, and two or three young men were engaged in what looked like a drug deal.

"Oh Marge, this is unbelievable. This is disgraceful. Isn't it a shame what people will do? Buildings deteriorate, but they shouldn't be destroyed. The elements don't wreck cities, people do."

"Let's get out of here," my mother repeated.

"But what about your house?" I asked her. "We've come this far, don't you want to see it?"

"No," she answered. "Why would I want to see it ruined? It's a war zone. Let's go."

"And to think that just yesterday we were in a real war zone," my father lamented. "How can they spend all that money to preserve Antietam, a place where people died, then turn a place where people live into a battlefield?"

From the urban war zone we headed to the quiet cemetery in the nearby town of Totowa. Tom Leonard died in 1968, and after my dad went back for the funeral and saw what was happening to Paterson he decided to do something about it . . . in his mind. In the forty-some years since the funeral, my father rebuilt the city of his birth brick by brick. He restored the armory, repaved the streets, and rehabbed the houses, especially his, reclaiming everything that had been destroyed. Now he had to start all over again.

"Paterson, when I grew up, was a good middle-class city," Dad remarked as I steered the RV onto the Totowa exit ramp. "Clean streets. Good transportation. It was friendly. It was safe. We never had a key to our house. We never locked it."

"There had to be some criminals," I argued.

"They didn't come to our house," Dad replied.

"No," added my mother. "I don't know where they were."

We turned into the cemetery gate and parked along the shoulder of a narrow road, somewhere in the middle of the graveyard. It was a cold day, the yellowed grass covered here and there by small patches of icy snow. My father was confident that he could find the graves once he got acclimated to the surroundings and as he started his search, I walked over to where my mother was standing.

"I don't like cemeteries," she said, shuffling from foot to foot to stay warm. "They're depressing. I'm not going to stay out long. I'm going in . . . You too!"

She yelled the last few words toward my dad, who was moving farther and farther away.

"No!" he shouted back. "I have to see this."

Mom shook her head.

"I don't know where my father and sisters are," she said while starting to edge back toward the RVs. "I don't know . . . and I'm not going to walk all around here to find out."

Once again, my parents were going in opposite directions.

"What year was it when your dad died?" I asked, hoping the conversation would keep her from leaving.

"I don't remember when my dad died. I don't even remember coming to the cemetery . . . I guess I had to."

My mother shrugged and headed off to the Holiday Rambler. When I found my dad a few minutes later he was standing by a plain, rather new-looking headstone, talking to Brendan.

"There's my mother, Annie, my father, Thomas J., my sister Anna, my brother, Thomas F., and my mother's sister Catherine."

"So the last time you were here was when your father was buried?" I asked.

"Yep," he said, then turned and looked at the grave. After a long pause he turned back to us.

"Thank you . . . thank you . . . thank you for coming," he said quietly, a faraway look on his face as he stared toward the ground at our feet.

"There's something odd about this," I said, breaking the silence. "The gravestone . . . I don't know . . . it doesn't look old enough. Didn't you say he was buried in the late 'sixties?"

"Yeah," Dad replied, turning again to stare at the three-foot-high, beige stone.

The cold wind was starting to take its toll and I was about to suggest that we head back to the RV when I suddenly remembered something that my younger brother Kevin told me a long time ago. He had taken his wife and three children on a car trip through the East and had visited the Totowa cemetery. He too was curious about the headstone and took it upon himself to solve the mystery.

"I know what the deal is," I said to my father.

Dad turned to face me. I could see that the cold was getting to him as well. His face was red and his hands were trembling.

"Kevin told me the story," I said. "Remember when he came here with his family? He wondered about the gravestone too and, well, you know him, the answer had to be somewhere, so Kevin checked with the people in the cemetery office and they looked up the records. It seems that when your uncle Johnny Smith died he put something in his will about giving the Leonards a better gravestone. He wanted to thank your parents for opening their home to him when he came from Ireland and for all those other times through the years when they sheltered and fed him. I guess being a gravedigger gave him a certain perspective on the significance of headstones and when you think about it, the bigger marker is the perfect gift, because he didn't do it for the glory. He was dead. It was a present from the dead to the dead."

My father was dumbstruck, saying nothing as he slowly turned to look at the headstone one last time before leaving. The trembling in his hands, I noticed, had now spread to his lower lip.

We left the cemetery and drove to a small RV facility on the docks of Jersey City. It was late afternoon and large ferryboats filled with commuters from Manhattan were arriving at regular intervals, the Statue of Liberty looming behind them as they filed off with their briefcases and newspapers. I was alone, standing near the dock, looking out at the water and thinking about the day. There was a lot to digest: my father's fall, the college visit, Paterson, the headstone. My mother never did go looking for her father's grave, returning to the cemetery only briefly after Kerry found where Martin Curley and Bridget O'Halloran, her mother's parents, were buried.

I looked out at the Statue of Liberty. It triggered vague recollections of a childhood trip to New York with my brother Jack. We'd taken a boat ride around Manhattan and wondered why people were making such a big deal out of the huge green lady with a crown and torch. Now I was looking at it again but in a much different light. A half century had passed since that boyhood visit and as I now stared across the water, sparkling in the golden light from the setting sun, my mind drifted back to the cemetery in Totowa and the thought of how I had lingered by

Bridget O'Halloran's headstone as everybody else walked back to the RVs.

She was the reason we were there.

It was Bridget O'Halloran's engagement ring, saved for decades in a jewelry box by her daughter Margaret, my grandmother, that allowed me to buy a movie camera. That movie camera led to a job in TV, and that job gave me the freedom to make this trip happen. A dead person's gift, this time to the living, set in motion by an amazing set of circumstances that now, more than ever, seem to fit some kind of pattern. My grandmother handed a small diamond ring to the man who offered her shelter, my father, who then entrusted it to a total stranger, a female flight attendant, who carried it fifteen hundred miles to the arrival lounge at O'Hare, where a college kid in blue jeans and a T-shirt was waiting. She gave him the ring, a hug, and a wish for happiness.

It had come true.

"When you heard that he died, what did you feel?"

"Nothing."

It was later in the evening, and I was asking my mom about her father. She had always danced around my questions, making little jokes or changing the subject entirely. I knew there were problems, that he gambled and drank, that my grandmother was left with few assets, that he wasn't friendly . . . but those were generalities. Yet Mom's behavior at the cemetery, her refusal to look for her own father's grave, had impelled me to ask more pointed questions. And for the first time in my life, she was ready with answers.

"You felt no sadness when he died?"

"No," she said. "Isn't it awful to say? But he was mean. He was mean to my mother. You lived in fear. I'd be up at two A.M. looking out the window and then I'd say to my mom, 'Here he comes.' "

We were sitting in the Holiday Rambler, Mom and Dad facing each other at the dinette table, Matt and I sitting side by side on the couch. The others had gone back to the Winnebago to watch a DVD.

"She had a sinus operation once and her nose was all bandaged," my mother said while wiping her makeup off with a piece of Kleenex. "He came home drunk and punched her in the nose. I was there."

"And your mother was the greatest, nicest, classiest woman in the world!" Dad exclaimed, shaking his head. "But she couldn't invite people into the house. Marge could never tell her father that she was a cheerleader. He wouldn't have allowed it. She had to hide her megaphone in the bushes and say she was going to the library. Same with the elevator operator job at the department store, Quackenbush's, that wouldn't have been allowed either."

"We were always afraid," Mom said. "I was glad when he was gone. He did give me money, though . . ."

"But he didn't give you love," interrupted my father.

"Did you miss that?" I asked.

"I didn't really know at the time," she replied. "Not until later in life."

While my mother paused to take a sip of her wine, I tried to imagine what it was like to carry that heavy load through life . . . and to do it in silence, at least in the company of her young children.

"He wouldn't be there on Christmas morning," my mother continued. "He'd be gone. I don't know where he was."

"Would you give him a present?" I asked.

"Yeah. He wouldn't open it. It just stayed under the tree. I think my mother would finally put his presents up in his room or something, I don't know. He never opened mine."

"And this went on after your older sisters moved out?" I asked. "When it was just you, your mom, and your dad?"

She nodded.

"I don't get why somebody wouldn't open a little girl's Christmas present!" I exclaimed. "What does that prove?"

"I don't know," Mom replied. "I got used to it. I don't know what was wrong with him."

That last line struck me. Something was wrong with **him**, not her. Children of abusive parents often point the finger at themselves, believing that they are somehow to blame. My mom took a different course of action.

"I hit him with a chair once," she said in a calm voice. "My mother needed money for something, groceries, something little. He wouldn't give it to her. I was about nine years old and was holding on to her leg. I was afraid to leave my mother's side, thinking he might hurt her. She kept telling me to go in the other room, but I wouldn't leave. Finally I'd had enough. She was still asking for the money and he was still refusing. I walked over to the other side of the room, picked up a big, heavy dining-room chair . . . I don't know how I lifted it . . . then came at him from behind and smashed it over his head. He crashed to the floor and I took off, running out of the house to a hiding place in the alley. I was afraid he was going to kill me, but instead he went off and got drunk or something. I can't remember."

Young Marge.

Men who show bravery in combat are often honored with ribbons and medals, sometimes even parades. Their obituaries are filled with glowing descriptions of courage in the face of hostile fire. When my mom dies, there won't be any such praise. A nine-year-old girl armed with a dining-room chair is not the stuff of legend. A woman who falls on a psychological grenade to protect her children from emotional harm is never saluted as a conquering hero. Scan the horizon for my mother's mark and you'll see nothing but flat, smooth ground. There won't, however, be a hole. She filled that up. And that's her monument.

The Leonard boys got an even start in life. We didn't have to boost ourselves from a pit of self-pity. There was no tiptoeing around a moody, resentful mother laid low by an unhappy childhood. My mom took the hole left by her father and used it as burial place, dumping in the bad memories, then covering them up with her feisty, humorous behavior. It couldn't have been easy. A hole that huge can take a lifetime to fill completely. Maybe that explains my mother's nightly nips from the bottle. Maybe that's the reason for her overwrought fears of physical harm. Whatever the cause . . . it's understandable.

Now.

Thirteen

"The George Washington Bridge!" Dad called out. "Once the longest suspension bridge in the world."

It was the nineteenth of February, a Thursday morning, and our convoy of two was approaching the entrance to the massive structure connecting New Jersey to New York. The double-deck bridge, almost four thousand feet long with a dozen lanes on each level, rises 250 feet above the Hudson River. I stopped the Holiday Rambler at the tollgate and glanced to the back to see how you-know-who was doing. Mom was sitting on the couch with a coat draped over her head. She hates bridges, heights, highway driving, and now me for combining all of those fearsome elements into one experience. What was I supposed to do, fly her over the river? That wouldn't work: She hates flying most of all.

"I remember the day the bridge opened," Dad continued. "I think it was 1931. At about ten in the morning, my father says, 'Hey Jack, let's you and I go over to see the George Washington Bridge.' And I said, 'Aw gosh . . .'—there was something going on that I wanted to attend. 'No,' he says, 'this is something you'll never forget.' And so we went over the bridge, went around a couple blocks in New York City, made another turn, and came back over and went home. The toll was fifty cents. I think you only paid one way. The theme was . . . this would make enough money in two or three years to pay the cost of the bridge and then it would be free. What did we pay this morning, twelve dollars? That doesn't sound free to me."

"Yeah, but we're kind of like a truck," I said from the driver's seat. "So we pay a higher fee . . . something to do with how many axles. I think it costs cars around six bucks. I guess they have to keep charging a toll because of maintenance and security. A lot of work has been done since the 'thirties, a second deck and lots of structural stuff."

Dad shook his head. "Yeah, but . . ."

"Son of a bitch . . . are we over the damn thing yet?"

My father's reply had been cut short by the agitated voice coming from beneath the coat.

"We're almost there!" I yelled back to my hooded mother, flipping roles in the timeworn script of the American family car trip. "There" meant the other side of the bridge, where Route 95 turns north then east, up the Connecticut coastline toward our destination: Providence, Rhode Island, three hours away. It was the end of the line, the farthest we would go before turning back and heading for home. The original plan called for a stop in New London before proceeding on to Providence, but we switched the order because the Providence College hockey team was leaving town that night and I wanted to catch a bit of their afternoon practice before they shipped off for a weekend series in Maine. Another reason for the switch had to do with Brendan's desire to visit some of his college buddies, all of them active participants in a curious anthropological movement to restructure the weekly calendar.

"Brendan wants to see his friends tonight because it's Thursday," I said during a short refueling break, everyone gathered in the Holiday Rambler.

"Why Thursday?" my mother inquired.

"Because that's the night everybody goes out," Brendan replied.

"What happened to Friday?" she asked.

"Thursday's the new Friday," Kerry responded.

My father scratched his head. "What are you talking about?" he said. "Thursday's Thursday."

"Not with college kids," Kerry noted. "Thursday's Friday now."

"Who the hell decided that?" asked Dad.

"Probably the same fool who ruled that it wasn't cool to sit down at a concert," I said. "If everybody sat they could all see the same thing. Try it, Brendan. Sitting is really comfortable. That's why they call tickets **seats** and not **stands**."

"Man," said Brendan, "do you sound old."

"And another thing . . ." I began.

"Uh-oh," groaned Matt. "I think I know what's coming next."

"Why does everybody wait until eleven at night to go out?" I continued. "What do you do from six until eleven?"

"I don't know, just hang out, kill time." Brendan replied. "Maybe take a nap. Nothing, really."

"So then why don't you go out at six?" I argued. "The places wouldn't be crowded or noisy . . . and you could find a place to sit."

Brendan shook his head. "When we get home I'm going to TiVo you a whole season of **Matlock**."

Up the coast we went, passing through Stamford, Bridgeport, and Milford before hitting the outskirts of New Haven. My father's internal jukebox had been silent for a while. Then he saw the sign: Yale University.

"Boola Boola, boola boola, boola boola, boola boola . . ."

After crooning the nonsensical lyrics he chuckled to himself. "You'd think a bunch of smart guys could come up with better lyrics for their fight song," he said. "That thing makes no sense."

"Maybe it's got a deep meaning," I suggested. "Maybe we're too stupid to figure it out."

"I doubt it," Dad replied. "Some of the dumbest guys I knew were the smartest. Marge, you remember that neighbor of ours, Chadwick or Duckworth or whatever his name was, you know that stuck-up guy who thought . . ."

"Oh yeah," Mom chimed in, "a real dope . . . had all that family money and was tighter than a frog's ass."

I waited a beat.

"And that's watertight!" they both exclaimed in unison, acting as if I had slept through the previous ten thousand recitations of that same, tired punch line.

We arrived at Providence College in time to watch the last half hour of hockey practice from the bench area close to the ice. The coaches knew me and when they skated over individually to say a quick hello, I introduced them to my parents and joked about feeling old in the presence of such young, quick players.

"Faster players, faster life," quipped Rick Bennett, an assistant coach who once played in the NHL.

"Yeah," joked Dave Berard, another coach. "You always remember yourself better than you were."

"Maybe **you** do," I replied. "Not me."

In 1965, my options for the future were limited. Poor grades and low scores on the college entrance exams had dashed any hopes of playing Division One college hockey, despite my rapid improvement in the sport after a late start as a high school sophomore. The solitary early-morning skating sessions and the exposure to knowledgeable coaches fueled a rapid rise to the top line on the top team in the state. My line mates, Jim McNerney and Dave Gurley, were good players, and the three of us succeeded by skating hard and passing the puck to whoever happened to be open. We didn't try to be individual stars, and that's exactly what made us stars . . . in Illinois.

In the mid-1960s, big-time college hockey programs had no interest in players from the Midwest. The scarcity of indoor facilities and fluctuating winter temperatures kept our season short. All of the proven talent was coming from Massachusetts, Rhode Island, Minnesota, and, of course, Canada. Why would a college coach take a chance on an unseen player from a suspect hockey state, especially a player with lousy grades? They didn't. All of my applications were rejected, including the one sent to Providence College.

I was at the crossroads. One non–hockey-playing school had accepted me, but going there would mean giving up the only activity in which I showed promise. Or was it promise? Not according to the experts, and they certainly must know, being experts.

In fact, they didn't even have to see me play to reach that conclusion. The formula was in place. It was rock solid. Illinois kids don't have the skills. That was the conventional wisdom. Jack and Marge, thank God, are anything but conventional.

"What about Lake Forest Academy?" Dad had suggested.

"Huh?" I responded.

"It's a prep school," he replied.

The only thing I knew about prep school was that JFK had gone to one, leading me to assume that they existed solely as a launching pad for well-bred Eastern brainiacs bound for Harvard. My father explained that Lake Forest Academy was a highly regarded boarding school that allowed for a certain number of day students. And it was only a twenty-minute car ride from our house in Glencoe. And . . . it had a hockey team.

"You could live at home," he said. "Go to school to get your grades up, play for the LFA team and your old team at the same time. You could be on two teams. That's a lot of extra practice. Then you could give college another try next year."

"So . . . is it sort of like a junior college?" I asked.

"No. It's still high school. You'd have to repeat your senior year."

"A second senior year of high school?" I stammered. "People would think I flunked!"

"Who cares?" he said. "Hughie Brower told me

about the place. I already called them. The entrance exam is on Saturday morning."

"An entrance exam? Oh shit."

I bombed the test but Mr. McClellan, the dean of students and a good guy, showed mercy, and the acceptance letter arrived in the mail a few weeks later. In certain circles back east, an extra postgraduate year of prep school study wasn't as foreign a concept as it was to us Midwesterners, at least back then. I was dating Cathy at the time. Let me rephrase that . . . Cathy was allowing me to take her to an occasional movie and dinner as long as I didn't try to put my arm around her shoulder or otherwise humiliate her in public. She was preparing to head off to Milwaukee's Marquette University and was as confused as everyone else upon learning that I was pointed in the opposite direction—back toward high school.

Loyola Academy didn't fail me; I failed it by ducking behind as many heads as I could, an easy path to anonymity in a big school. There were no such hiding places at Lake Forest Academy. With six or seven students in each classroom, everything I said or did was noticed. Even my absentminded doodling was observed, an oddly encouraging development for someone who could only stare at his shoes when called upon to contribute. Those shoes, by the way, were an old pair of tan bucks worn so often that most of the buck material had rubbed off, leaving behind a dark, semi-shiny surface. While zoning out in class one day, I used my pen to draw lines and dots on both shoes, a quasi-artistic flight of fancy that turned my worn-out bucks into imitation wingtips.

"Hey Leonard, those shoes are cool."

"Huh? These shoes? My shoes?"

"Hey guys, look at Leonard's shoes."

An aspect of my personality that had once been categorized as a weakness—my habitual daydreaming—was being viewed as a strength. I had always been a perceptive observer of everyday life, noting the small, unimportant details that everybody else seemed to miss. Now I was picking up on the bigger stuff and the masses, surprisingly, were still missing it. A top student, for instance, would solve a blackboard full of mathematical equations, then come unglued when someone else got a higher grade or was accepted to a more prestigious college. It was as if the stain of failure would forever tarnish his family name. For a serial flunky such as myself, the realization of knowing more about life than the supposed genius was encouraging.

Then hockey started.

Playing with Mike Hall and Doug Read on the top line of a team that lost only once added another dimension to my persona at the small school. Teachers would go to the games and make favorable comments about my play the next day in class. I wasn't used to hearing any kind of praise in an academic setting and even though it was hockey that drew the kudos, the positive feedback lessened my knee-jerk desire to duck for cover. So I couldn't diagram a sentence? Nobody else in the class appeared to know as much as I did about bouncing back up, a far more relevant subject, it seemed.

While playing for Lake Forest Academy, I was also skating for a team comprised of the best players in the Chicagoland area, reuniting with Jim McNerney and Dave Gurley on the number-one line. Jim and Dave had been a year behind me in school, and this extra chance to blend back in with talented and unselfish linemates improved my game while hammering home the point about the pitfalls of glory seeking. Our coach, Chet Stewart, was a fanatic about staying in position, moving the puck to the open man and digging deep to slog through the unglamorous parts of the game for the good of the team. By the end of the season, the benefits of skating seven days a week, sometimes twice a day, was showing. On the academic side, my grades and college test scores were still mediocre at best but I knew a lot more, especially about myself. Feeling good about the future, I reapplied to the same hockey-playing colleges that had rejected me the previous spring.

And they rejected me again.

Every single one of them.

Now what?

"I have an idea," my father said.

"Not another year of high school," I sighed.

No, this was a new plan, inspired by the fact that one of the rejecting schools, Providence College, was under the direction of the Dominican Friars, a Catholic religious order. In 1942, after being sent by the Navy for training in Florida, my father acted on the recommendation of a family friend and went to visit a church in Miami. He wore his white uniform, and while he was kneeling in a pew the parish priest, Monsignor Barry, a native of Ireland, tapped him on the shoulder and asked in a good-natured way what a Navy man was doing at a women's prayer service. They talked afterward and Monsignor Barry introduced my dad to a visiting Dominican Friar, Father Burk. Stories were shared, a friendship developed, and the three men kept in touch by letter after my father shipped out to sea.

Now it was twenty-five years later, and the search was on for that friendly Friar. If he were still alive, so were my chances.

He was.

My father called Father Burk, who called his Dominican cohort at Providence, who called the school's athletic director, who called me, paging my name over O'Hare's loudspeaker as I waited with McNerney, Gurley, and the rest of my high school–age teammates to fly out of Chicago for a national tournament.

"Hello Mike, this is Father Begley, athletic director at Providence College. I understand that you are on your way to the nationals and I thought you might skate a bit faster knowing that we have approved your application. Welcome to Providence College."

It seemed as if somebody hit a mute button, deadening every bit of sound at the busy airport. I saw myself from above . . . standing there in the silence, a red phone in my hand, a shocked expression on my face. Everywhere around me people were hustling this way and that, not one of them even the slightest bit curious about why the dizzy kid on the phone seemed incapable of saying a word.

Father Begley finished the conversation by explaining that academic probation would be in effect for the duration of my first year. It didn't matter to me, and in September of 1966, carrying two canvas hockey bags stuffed with my belongings, I arrived on the all-male campus of Providence College never having seen the place. The room assignments were alphabetical: Leggett, Lenczycki, Leonard—Room 321, Aquinas Hall. The narrow, winding staircase was filled with people lugging trunks and suitcases. This was the pre–"rent a U-Haul and bring everything" era. There were no microwaves, mini refrigerators, TV sets, DVD players, game systems, computers, printers, or cell phones . . . just a bunch of strangers, some of them stepping aside to let the awed kid with lots of baggage work his way up the stairs.

I didn't know what to fear more—being over-whelmed in the classroom or on the rink. One flunked course and you were gone. A few bad prac-tices and **sayonara**. The school had nothing invested in me. I was a charity case. With the Vietnam War in full swing, all able-bodied, unmarried males under the age of twenty-five not taking a full schedule of courses in a four-year college were eligible for the draft. Flunk a few college tests and six months later you could be dodging bullets in the jungles of South-east Asia.

The academic stuff was a challenge, but since there were no major exams early on, I didn't really know how to judge my standing. The grading process in hockey would be different. You can't hide weak skating or timid play, a thought that made me nervous as I walked into the locker room for the first time. Stuck above each set of equipment was a name written in black felt-tip ink on white tape, a very re-movable, very temporary reminder that not every-body listed would still be there a few days later. Jean Boislard was speaking French to Brian Smiley. Skip Sampson took out his teeth. Jimmie Murphy chatted up the big guy next to him in a heavy Rhode Island accent. They were all freshmen. Until the early 1970s, the NCAA didn't allow first-year college stu-dents to play a varsity sport. That would help my odds . . . unless Illinois hockey was as bad as every-one said it was.

It wasn't.

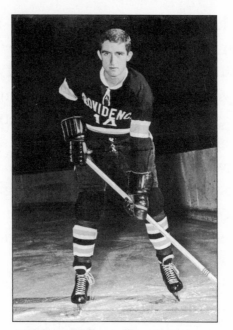

College boy on ice.

I made the freshman team and finished the season tied for second in scoring. Our coach, a young firebrand named Lou Lamoriello, valued the style of play that had been drilled into me during high school. Skate hard. Win the little battles. Be a team player. It's an uncomplicated formula, yet some players couldn't seem to figure out why it should apply to them. Off they'd go in search of hero's glory, flying around the ice in grand displays of wasted motion, gaining nothing from their flamboyance but a seat on the bench. Those players came from hockey hotbeds. They were the ones who were supposed to make it in college hockey, not me.

It was another defining revelation. If I had followed

the advice of the experts, I would have eliminated myself from the running. Why waste time trying, after all, when the voices from above proclaim your cause to be lost? Could those voices be wrong? Absolutely. But how would you know if you had listened and quit?

I played hockey all through college. The varsity team had hit the skids and because of Lou Lamoriello's success as a freshman coach, he had been moved up to lead the varsity squad. He was as tough as they come and never, ever let up. It was all about effort. No excuses. Just go out there and bust your ass. That's difficult to do on a losing team, the temptation being to find solace in moral victories, patting yourself on the back for keeping it close. That attitude didn't fly with Lou, especially on a cold December night in my senior year.

The best player on our team, Rich Pumple, a big, tough junior from Lachine, Quebec, had broken his leg in the previous game. He was our leader, the main reason to believe that the play-offs were within reach. When he was put on a stretcher and carried off the ice, those play-off hopes went with him. Our next game was against a far superior Brown University team, playing at their home rink, always a boisterous environment. After two periods Brown was leading 3–1, and Lou sensed what was on our minds. With our most skilled athlete out of the picture, a close loss to a great team would be a victory of sorts.

Oh, no, it wouldn't.

Minutes before we were to hit the ice for the final period, Lou burst into the locker room. In a rage he picked up a big, metal garbage can and hurled it against the wall. Then he started screaming. And screaming. Everybody in the world has an excuse for failing, he hollered, everybody in every situation has something or someone to blame for falling short.

The supplies didn't arrive in time.
The phone call wasn't returned.
Somebody screwed up the order.

Bullshit.
We were missing a great player; too bad. Life is full of unlucky breaks.
Get over it.
Find a way.
Buried somewhere in the college hockey archives there is a date and a score:

December 18, 1969
Providence College 5–Brown University 3.

In the grand scheme of things, a midseason game won decades ago by a college hockey team that never amounted to much is a trivial matter. Unless, of course, you happened to be in the visitor's locker room that night, heard the speech, saw what followed, and then realized how much more is possible with a little extra push.

As for not being able to compete in the classroom, well, the experts were also wrong about that. I did fine, taking advantage of the academic freedom to load up on liberal arts courses while steering clear of as much math and science as possible.

Most of my classmates had campus jobs and so did I, as a food server in the dining hall and as a maintenance man for the baseball field. Summer breaks were spent in Chicago, first doing janitorial work at Marina City, a high-rise apartment complex, and then jackhammering the Lake Shore Drive pavement with a city construction crew. My parents had moved to Scottsdale, Arizona, prior to my sophomore year in college and wanted me to spend the summers with them, but there was better money to be made in Chicago, even if it meant dishing out fourteen bucks a week for my small room at the Evanston YMCA. Money, however, wasn't the real reason for staying in Chicago. Cathy was. She liked me now. Finally.

It was my greatest triumph: humoring the smart, pretty girl into taking me seriously. We had always gotten along well, laughing and talking our way through teenhood. She just had somebody different in mind for a boyfriend, somebody a little more . . . substantial. I blame JFK. Cathy had gotten swept away by the hoopla surrounding the 1960 presidential election and it screwed up the settings on her boyfriend detector. After the inauguration, nothing moved the needle except for touch-football-playing preppies with Boston accents, good grades, gleaming teeth, sailing experience, and about four hundred cousins. Enter me. Lousy student. No cousins. Braces. I did have a connection to yachting if you count the Ivory Soap sailboat carved in Cub Scouts. Cathy didn't count that but remained friendly, using me as an escort service of sorts while tracking the westerly movement of all males leaving Hyannisport.

Then something happened. The needle moved. I had invited Cathy to a classmate's party near the end of my second senior year. To the outside world, nothing about me seemed all that different. The nose was still bent and broken, the academic standing still shaky, despite my higher class rank. Lake Forest Academy listed me at number fifty-four, an impressive figure unless you happened upon a yearbook and counted heads on the senior picture page. Fifty-four heads.

I was still last.

I just wasn't lost.

The small-school environment had shone a light in my direction, illuminating the tiniest fragments of creativity. With a new layer of confidence protecting my dented psyche, I found the courage to move forward in an eccentric but hopeful direction. Thank God Cathy liked where I was headed.

Later that summer we started to get serious about each other, and for the next three years our daily letters crisscrossed the airways between Providence and Milwaukee. Face time was limited to about a week in

Cathy in front of her Glencoe, Illinois, home in 1969.

the spring and three months in summer, as hockey kept me on campus during every Thanksgiving break and all but five days of the Christmas vacation. Cathy graduated in 1969, a year ahead of me, and on the night before heading back to Providence for my senior year I stopped my car on a quiet street in our little hometown and gave Cathy a piece of gum. Inside the wrapper was Bridget O'Halloran's ring.

We were engaged.

The wedding was set for June 20, 1970. Most of our nest egg had been spent on the movie camera and a Bermuda honeymoon package, but having little money in the bank wasn't a big concern. Why save for our future, after all, when our future was in the hands of Uncle Sam?

The Vietnam War was still raging and to cut down on bogus deferments, especially by college kids, the Department of Defense had instituted a draft lottery, based on birthdates, in November of 1969. My number, 174, wasn't high enough to put me in the clear, so I drove into downtown Providence, parked my car, walked into the first recruiting station that came into sight, the Air Force, and signed up. It was the standard arrangement for second-semester seniors, calling for a group physical, which I passed, followed by the arrival of orders sometime after graduation.

Everybody on campus was affected one way or another by the war situation. Guys with high lottery numbers had a free pass to the next phase of their life while the rest were either committed to the military or stuck in a holding pattern, waiting for a letter from the draft board that could very well spell their doom. In many cases, mine included, it was useless to plan a career while we bided our time. Our fate belonged to a stranger. And wouldn't you know it—the stranger writing my ticket had a sense of compassion.

He came into my life on a routine walk across campus in early March. John Sanford, a hockey teammate, had joined me for a mid-afternoon trip to the school cafeteria. Halfway there we ran into the college ROTC commander, a middle-aged military officer and a hockey fan. He asked about our plans and when I mentioned the Air Force obligation, my friend John shook his head and quietly mumbled a few words to himself, still expressing surprise that I'd passed the physical. The ROTC man asked for details and I gave him a brief description of my curved spine, how it had caused a lifetime of back problems but not enough to merit an attempt to escape military service since I had always managed to play hockey through the pain.

The uniformed officer then took a pad out of his pocket, wrote the name and phone number of a local doctor, looked me in the eye, and told me to make an appointment. I put my hand out and he repeated the request before letting go of the paper. It was a bizarre encounter—a career military man seemingly offering safe passage to a young man who just happened by. I followed his instructions. The doctor x-rayed my back but said nothing other than to ask for my mailing address. A short time later, U.S. forces expanded the war into Cambodia, campus protests erupted across the land, and in the violence that followed, students at Kent State and Jackson State were gunned down.

What followed was surreal. Providence College, like many schools, had called off the last month of classes. We waited around for graduation, then said good-bye to our college years and each other, not knowing how the rest of the script would play out. The letter from the U.S. Department of Defense arrived one week before my wedding. I opened it slowly.

"Registrant not qualified for any military service, 4F."

What if I hadn't run into the ROTC commander on the walk across campus? What if my friend and teammate hadn't muttered his surprise about the physical? Between the time of my rejection letter and the 1972 pullout of U.S. troops, approximately four thousand additional Americans died in Vietnam. Roughly thirty-five thousand more were wounded. Those facts I know. What I don't know is the name of that campus military man.

Two paths cross, and somebody's life changes.

But why my life?

And why so often?

Those thoughts were on my mind as I steered the Holiday Rambler past the college gates and toward the nearby highway that would lead us to our campsite. When we got there, I took my cell phone outside and called Cathy. It was a beautiful night, the winter sky full of bright stars. For the first thirty seconds of the conversation Cathy managed to put on a brave front. Her intent was to shield me from worry, but we know each other too well and her tears came quickly. Megan had just received the results from her final ultrasound.

Something might be wrong with the baby.

Fourteen

The ultrasound revealed that Megan's baby hadn't gained weight in a month. The medical people said that it could be the sign of a serious condition or it could be nothing. Meg chose to believe the latter and tried to reassure Cathy by explaining how her doctor would have intervened if a true crisis were looming. I agreed with Megan's philosophy, but part of Cathy's fear had wormed its way into my thought process. All four of our children were healthy. Our lives were blessed. Perhaps too blessed?

The next morning we circled back to Providence to pick up Brendan, who had slept in one of the dorms. New London was an easy drive to the south, and on the way my parents were full of talk about the old Navy town that had served as their home during most of World War II. I hadn't told anyone about the situation with Megan and Jamie's baby. Nobody needed the worry—certainly not my mom and dad, and certainly not in New London, where their own baby is buried.

She died sixty years ago. That's about all I know. A lifetime of questions had been avoided.

Until now.

"I put the crib up," Dad began, "and had all the things you had to have for a new baby and never gave a thought that things wouldn't turn out great. Well, let me tell you, when it didn't turn out just right, it was one helluva shock."

"Oh no, you don't forget it," Mom said. "No. No. That baby had a bad heart. In those days they couldn't fix things like they do today."

"It was full term," Dad added. "We did all the things prescribed. We thought everything would be fine. The doctors in New London were just great. The chaplain on the base was very good. We didn't know too many people, but everybody was kind. My feeling of life is, the greatest thing you can do for other people is show kindness. Show some kindness."

"Have you been back to the grave?" I asked.

"No," Dad answered as Mom nodded her head in agreement, "but if we went there now we would find a tombstone with our child's name on it. We named the baby Ann, after my mother."

"That's why I worry all the time," Mom continued. "I think of . . . you know . . . God forbid, but I'll be glad when Megan has this baby and it's over. Everything's okay, right?"

"Yep," I replied. "Everything's fine."

It was late in the morning when we exited Route 95 and followed the signs to the New London beaches. My parents were certain that once we found our way to Ocean Avenue, it would be easy to locate the house they'd shared with three other Navy couples.

"That's it!" my mother exclaimed. "That's it, right there with the red roof."

The house was a big, rambling structure just up the hill from a narrow inlet. I parked the RV and helped my mom and dad step down to the quiet street. Holding hands, they walked a few short steps to the far curb and looked up in silence at the large home on the corner lot.

"Oh, they were the nicest people we ever knew." My father sighed.

"Yeah, great," nodded my mom. "Wonderful."

"Especially Dave Connole," said Dad. "He was the skipper of a submarine called 'The Trigger.' Before he left he gave me his Naval Academy bathrobe, which I kept for twenty years."

"Dave left about two weeks after their little baby

was born," Mom said. "A little baby boy. I'd go out with his wife, Vida, and we'd walk around New London and she'd see admirals who had just come back and she'd ask if they knew anything about 'The Trigger,' and they might have known but they said they didn't. It was missing. Well, I happened to be home and I didn't see them come in. I heard a lot of commotion because they lived right above us and I heard crying and I thought something was wrong so I kind of went out in the hall and I saw the chaplain leave. Then I went up to see her and it was horrible. I guess a kamikaze got the whole ship and they were all gone."

Of the four Navy men in the house only one, my father, returned from the sea.

It was a cold, cloudy day. After leaving the house we drove to the beach where my mom had spent many of her days, scanning the watery horizon for the first glimpse of a returning ship. We wheeled the RV close to the boardwalk and stepped out into the icy wind blowing in from the ocean. My parents walked slowly away from the group and stood by themselves, holding hands once again while staring in silence at the open water.

By mid-afternoon we were settled into our slots in the nearby campground. I did my exercises while the others busied themselves with laundry and postcard writing. Brendan took a nap, catching up on the sleep he'd missed on his Thursday-night romp. The

Naval Officer Jack

sun was starting to set when I interrupted my father's
game of solitaire to ask him about the men in the
house, the war, and his own experiences at sea.

"For most of the war, I was the skipper of a small
escort ship," he began. "German submarines were
sinking lots of our supply vessels, and it was our duty
to try and protect them from the subs."

"Did anybody get killed on your ship?" I asked.

"Not on the ship itself," my father replied. "But
death was all around. You had to get used to it. We
picked up a guy in the water one time. He must
have gotten washed overboard or blown off some
ship. No identification papers . . . looked to be in
his early twenties . . . not American. He died right
after we pulled him out. I remember walking to the
back of the ship and the doctor was sitting on a
piece of machinery sewing the guy into what we
called a sail bag. It was made out of canvas with
some stuff put in there to weight it down. As the
doctor stitched up the bag he was singing 'By the
Light of the Silvery Moon.' No emotion . . . almost
like he was sewing up a torn shirt. I said a prayer
over the man in the bag and we put him on a plank,
tipped it down, and he slid into the ocean. Some
mother somewhere was probably praying for years
hoping for her son to come home. She never found
out why he didn't . . . or how he died . . . or where.

"We were part of a huge convoy once, at least two
hundred ships," he continued. "And one of them de-

veloped engine trouble and had to drop out of the line. My ship got the order to go back and circle them . . . to give protection until they got their engine fixed. The sun was going down and it was starting to get dark and they still hadn't gotten it fixed. The signal came to leave them and rejoin the convoy. Those were the rules. The convoy stops for nothing. It was too dangerous. German subs were out there watching us. If the convoy slowed down, or split up, the U-boats would have had a field day, picking off the supply ships and the ammunition ships. So I had to leave."

My father took his hat off and put it next to him on the dinette table. He ran a hand through his white hair, paused for a few seconds, then picked up where he'd left off.

"About a half hour later there was a big boom. A German sub got them with a torpedo. We could see the glow from the fire. Imagine you're on a ship and it gets hit and starts to sink and you jump overboard thinking that there are two or three hundred friendly ships in the area . . . one of them will come to the rescue . . . and you wait, and nobody does. You're in the water and you're saying to yourself, 'My God, there was a ship circling us a half hour ago, it'll come back. It has to.' And it doesn't. And it's getting dark. And you realize that you're alone in the Atlantic and you're going to die there . . . young men like Matt and Brendan."

Dad turned his head and looked through the side window. There was no more to be said. The man who lives to help people was helpless when people needed him the most.

I stepped outside the Holiday Rambler and walked across the campsite to where the Winnebago was parked. Matt, Margarita, Kerry, and Brendan were inside passing the time until dinner. Kerry had talked to Megan on the phone and now they knew what I knew. We all agreed that it would be best to keep it from my parents, a difficult, if not impossible, task given my mother's uncanny ability to sniff out the truth.

"She's got the best act in the world," Kerry remarked. "She just sort of plays that innocent, dumb 'I don't know what's going on' act, but behind that veneer the wheels are turning."

"Dad knows what's going on too," I said. "But then he disregards what he knows and walks right back into an ass kicking. Down he goes, only to get up again . . . and again . . . and again. Meanwhile my mother has the binoculars out, looking down the road for the danger spots. She knows right where they are . . . and who they are. She's got the vision. He's got the resilience."

"The two of them are the yin and the yang of the human spirit," said Kerry. "And somehow they stayed connected."

"An interesting thing happened after the Paterson

visit," added Margarita. "I was sitting next to your mom at dinner and she started talking about her father, nothing specific, just saying how he was difficult. 'No wonder I'm crazy,' she said. I told her to look around the table. 'Maybe your childhood was bad,' I said, 'but look what you have now.' She got her Kleenex out. I think she was crying."

"That happened?" I asked. "My mother hardly ever cries in front of people. At least she doesn't around me."

We started reminiscing about the journey, how implausible the idea seemed at first, then the crash, the good scenery, the bad scenery, the funny times and annoying moments, agreeing that despite some ups and down, my parents seemed to have had a memorable ride.

"It's amazing," I said. "Mom and Dad are characters . . . crazy characters when you think about it. But they led pretty remarkable lives. Once they pass on though, who, outside of our family and a few friends, would even know they ever existed?"

"That's true," nodded Matt. "In world history, their footprint is nonexistent, but for us it's pretty large and will always be large."

Brendan stopped strumming his guitar. "Napoleon meant nothing to me," he said. "What does he have to do with me? You can say that about anyone. If you try to say, 'What am I worth to the entire world?' you're not going to be worth a whole lot. So, why don't you make yourself worth something to the people around you and the people you care about?

"It's weird to say that they're going to die sooner than I realize. And when that day comes I'll probably look back and say I wish I could have had, you know, a little more time with them. But I feel that since I'm on this trip it's almost as if I'm erasing that feeling of guilt when that day happens. And I think that I'm getting to know them a lot better as people rather than grandparents and I think it's worth it just for that. You know how Spoose always begins a story with 'so and so . . . the nicest guy you could ever meet.' He said this maybe twenty-five times about different people, and what I've slowly realized through this trip is that I think Spoose has been wrong about every single one of those people. They're not the nicest men I could ever meet because honestly I think my grandpa is probably the nicest man I could ever hope to meet. Just his attitude and his dealing with people and his openness and willingness to take people, you know, into his home and into his heart. I think that has kind of been an eye-opener for me, how kind my grandpa Spoose is."

While Brendan talked I leaned over to retie my shoelace, still trying to hide tears after fifty-six years of life.

Early the next morning Matt, Kerry, Brendan, and I headed off in the Winnebago while Margarita kept company with my parents in the Holiday Rambler. We had decided to look for Ann's grave, my children agreeing with my gut notion that it was best to keep my parents in the dark about the side trip. By asking the locals for directions we found the cemetery and within it, a section for babies. There were no tombstones marking the tiny graves, just small metal plaques, many of them covered over by soil and grass.

Grabbing a screwdriver from a box of tools in the Winnebago, I moved through the morning mist, from grave to grave, kneeling and scraping but never coming across a marker bearing the name of Ann Leonard. After an hour of searching, we flagged down a cemetery worker driving by in his truck. Paging through a site map he found Ann's name, but when he walked us to the plot the marker was nowhere to be seen.

"A lot of them get lost," he said in a thick New England accent. "If they get too high, the mower hits them and they're gone."

The middle-aged man in muddy coveralls was carrying a long metal rod, and he used it to scrape the outline of a small box onto the frozen yellow grass.

"So the baby's there?" I asked.

"The baby's definitely there," he replied.

The man walked back to his truck while the rest of us stared at the bare patch of ground. There was nothing to mark Ann Leonard's brief life. It was as if she'd never existed.

Two days later, the Chicago skyline came into view. The journey of a lifetime had gone by in the blink of an eye. Now we were approaching the end . . . and the beginning. Megan's due date was less than a week away, but the baby could come anytime. My parents were still unaware of the concern raised by the final ultrasound, although something in my mother's demeanor told me that she had once again detected a cause for worry. Was it justified? Not according to Megan. Our telephone conversations over the last few days had been upbeat. The baby would be fine, she said, and I agreed . . . on the phone. How could I tell her that my usual optimism had taken a hit in New London?

Sixty years earlier my parents had shared Megan's sense of hope. They expected everything to work out and it hadn't. Dad had set up the crib and while Mom was in labor he stood watch at the Naval hospital, an excited first-time father-to-be waiting to hand out cigars. A day later he was alone in the rented room, taking the crib down and packing away all other reminders of their high hopes.

What if Ann Leonard had lived? What if my mother had had a little girl to raise? What if my brothers and I had an older sister? Everything about us would be different. It's the factor of one. In the complex equation of life, a staggering number of human connections are made. All it takes is one . . . added or subtracted . . . and the final balance changes in ways impossible to calculate.

Those were my thoughts on the journey from New London to Chicago. Scary thoughts. Subtract just one of the many people who helped me through life and I would have stumbled badly. What if my grandmother hadn't given me the ring, or that priest in Miami hadn't tapped my father on the shoulder? What if that military man hadn't asked about my back? What if my friend in Phoenix hadn't encouraged me to try a new career?

After getting married in June of 1970, Cathy and I moved to Phoenix on a whim, having been suddenly set free by my unexpected military deferment. Nine months later Matt was born. Two and a half years after that, Megan arrived. While Cathy stayed home with the children, I went looking for a career to suit my soul. A strong inner sense of destiny, first realized at the Bob Dylan concert, had fueled a desire to search for something special. Lessons learned climbing the hockey ladder, coupled with the long struggle to gain acceptance into college, had forged my will to push beyond the inevitable rounds of rejection. To find a job that plays to your strengths, I knew that you first had to slog through the tasks that would highlight your weaknesses. Perseverance was the key.

As for the occupations that exposed my weaknesses, well, the list is long. Over an eight-year span I'd tried out for a professional hockey team, examined real-estate titles, worked construction, pounded the pavement as a salesman, toiled in retail, attempted sports management—and those are just the headliners. None of those professions fit. What I really did best was what I did just for fun: making movies with my Super 8 camera. The subjects, for the most part, were the members of my family. By capturing the fleeting moments of childhood on film, then splicing the scenes to a music soundtrack played on a separate tape recorder, I had found a way to slow down time. And I was being creative. Nothing suited me better.

"You should be doing that for a living," my friend Matt Sampson, an upstate New Yorker transplanted in Phoenix, had said.

"Making movies?" I replied. "Hollywood movies?"

"No," he answered. "Television. You're a storyteller. You should tell your stories on TV. You should be a feature reporter."

Me?

What about the nose, broken three more times in college? What about the unruly hair, long and curly? What about all the hemming and hawing, all the "you knows" and "umms" and "uhhs" sprinkled through every one of my sentences? Then there was the matter of my TV news experience: none. And the total number of journalism courses studied in school: zero. Oh yeah, and then there was my age. Thirty.

My friend Matt didn't bat an eye.

"You'd be great," he said with conviction.

And I believed him, despite the fact that he didn't work in TV. In fact, he didn't work at all. He was unemployed. A few days later, I was too. The time-consuming task of finding work in television required quitting work . . . but not my duties as a babysitter. Cathy had gone into labor with our third child, and on April 8, 1978, Kerry was born. Matt and Megan were psyched for the homecoming until I told them about the possibility of a slight delay. My shifting job status had left us without insurance and an unpaid balance of $500 was left on the hospital bill. The unsympathetic bean counter was playing hardball. They wanted their money before we left with our baby.

I went home that night feeling ashamed for putting the family into that kind of bind. The mailbox was empty except for a small envelope bearing no postage. When I opened it, my jaw dropped. It was $500 in cash. There was also a note filled with encouraging words and signed by my friend Matt . . . my unemployed friend Matt. I found out later that he had borrowed the money to keep me going.

After Cathy was back to feeling strong enough to care for our children, I began my final push for a TV job, lugging my projector around town hoping to impress the news directors with my creative handiwork. Their reaction instead seemed limited to utter bafflement as I went about stripping their office walls of framed pictures so I could use the white background as a screen for my home movies. Who let this guy in? All three network affiliates as well as the independent station turned me down, citing age, lack of experience, and no journalistic background as insurmountable obstacles. I had anticipated that response and countered with a spirited sermon about potential, creativity, and the willingness to work hard, but my words fell on deaf ears.

One chance remained. Early in my search for work, the co-owner of a local rock radio station, Eric Hauenstein, had allowed me to intern with the station's news director, a creative and fearless man named Mark Nykanen who saw something in me that others didn't. Mark had just left the radio side to try his hand at TV, signing on to anchor a low-budget public affairs show at a PBS station on the nearby campus of Arizona State University. I called Mark and a few days later was in his boss's office, taking down the pictures and switching on my projector. The man's name was Jim West, and I would like to say that Mr. West saw potential in my movies but

Four generations—
Margaret, Marge, Matt,
and Cathy.

Matt, Megan, Cathy,
and Kerry beat the
Phoenix heat.

Mike, Cathy,
and Kerry.

Mike and Brendan.

what he really saw, I'm sure, is desperation, and he showed pity by granting me a tryout.

I would be given one day's use of a cameraman and editor. I had four minutes to fill. The story subject was Ron Lee, a hyper-aggressive guard on the Phoenix Suns basketball team who tore through a pair of shoes per game. Put a story together in a compelling fashion, Mr. West said, and we'll take it from there. There were no instructions on how to get the player's cooperation or what kind of questions to ask or where to find the writing talent. But it was a sliver of daylight and I went for it, knowing that my only hope was to make the story unlike anything Jim West had seen. A quote from some self-help program stuck in my head:

Don't compete. Create.

How could I compete? I didn't have the training, the experience, or the looks. The only alternative was to create a new style. Be unique.

It worked. Jim West offered me a job. Using their cameramen, editors, and facilities, I would be required to research, report, write, and narrate two features stories per week. There was, however, a catch. My new position wasn't included in the budget. But Jim was kind. The petty-cash envelope usually contained about forty extra dollars at the end of every week. Jim said I could have it.

Forty bucks a week. Fifty hours of work. Even I could do the math. For less than a dollar an hour, a job in TV was mine for the taking. With a wife, three children, a mortgage, a car payment, and a bunch of other bills to pay . . . how could I refuse?

Cathy was great through it all. As the financial brains of our family she somehow kept us from the poorhouse, saving green stamps, clipping coupons, arranging for a $5,000 second mortgage, and so on. When our air conditioner blew out in the middle of summer, Al McLeod, a pro hockey–playing friend, loaned us the money to have it fixed. Our only other source of income was the weekly flea market, held in a stadium parking lot, where I would pay the five-dollar entry fee, open the back of our station wagon, then try to sell whatever could be spared from our dwindling list of possessions.

Only once, near the end of the third month, did Cathy ask if I had given any thought to the notion of looking for a better-paying job. The logic of my spontaneous answer surprised even me. If only we had an aerial view, I said, the prize would be clearly visible, sitting just around the next corner. But we were stuck at street level, our sightlines blocked by the tall trucks in front of us. With all the horns honking, there was no way to hear the people cheering us on from above . . . we wouldn't be able to hear their moans, either, if we ended up stopping a few feet short. It's there, right around the next corner, I know it is. Let's keep going.

A few weeks later I was hired as a part-time sports reporter at the local CBS station. The man doing the hiring at Channel 10, Bill Close, saw my tape and appreciated its unique style, never saying a word about my missing journalism degree, lack of experience, or age—deal breakers just three months earlier. Close, a Phoenix television legend, was the station's news director and main anchorman. He was also a blunt critic, never mincing words. I liked that, having learned from Lou Lamoriello, my college hockey coach, that hurt feelings often block the truth from seeping in. As a late starter—in hockey and television—I needed to get better faster, and those two men delivered lessons with a sonic boom, not that the sound wasn't startling at times.

The part-time reporting job paid a whopping $75 a week, with the promise of more to come if I earned full-time status, which happened a month later. The yearly salary was still low, in the $10,000 dollar range, and we were barely making ends meet. Midway through that year, the weekend sports-anchor position became available and I asked to be considered, simply for the money. The audition was somewhat intimidating: Read an old sports script into the unblinking eye of a studio camera set at close range. I did, and a few days later Bill Close called me into his office.

"We like you as a reporter," he said. "We think you have a future . . . as a reporter. You'll never be an anchor. You're too damn ugly." (He used a nastier word than "damn.")

I laughed.

"That's all right," I said. "I was just looking to make a little more money."

A few weeks later, with the weekend sports anchor now gone and no replacement under contract, Close called me to his office and asked if I could fill in on Saturday night.

"Sure," I replied. "Should I wear a bag over my face?"

Now he laughed.

Knowing that it was only a one-night temporary assignment gave me an extra boost of confidence to try something new. I can't remember how that different twist played out, but I do recall what happened afterward. The station's phones started ringing. Who was that guy with the messy hair, broken nose, and horrible delivery, asked the viewers. And . . . can we see more of him? Sometime later I was summoned to the office of the station owner, Tom Chauncey.

I knew what was up. They were going to offer me the main Monday-through-Friday sports anchor job. Cathy was hoping that the pay would be somewhere in the $25,000 range and when Mr. Chauncey told me the real figure, $22,000, he must have detected a slight look of disappointment.

"You don't seem that happy," he said.

"My wife was hoping for twenty-five thousand," I explained. "That would allow us to pay the people back."

"What people?" Mr. Chauncey asked.

"Oh, the second mortgage," I replied. "Some loans from friends . . . about eight thousand dollars in total."

"Come see me this afternoon," he said.

When I showed up he closed the door, walked to his desk, and took an envelope out of the top drawer.

"I'm still paying you twenty-two thousand," he said. "I don't want to get our salary structure out of whack. But this is a check to pay off your debts. It's ten thousand dollars and it's between us. Just promise to stay here for two years. Now get off your butt and go to Hanny's and charge five outfits to me—suits, sport coats, whatever. You need to start looking better."

The world around me was spinning. I was now the main sports anchor on the number-one station in town. And my family was free of debt. Soon afterward an ear, nose, and throat specialist operated on my battered and broken nose, clearing the air passages, chiseling down the huge lump, and making it straighter. That plus a bit of eyebrow plucking and presto, the mug was somewhat presentable. Hey, I was a TV anchor.

The **KOOL News** team: (left to right) Joe Doherty, Mary Jo West, Mike Leonard, and Bill Close.

But not for long.

The call came at home. Mr. Chauncey wanted to see me in his office right away. It was nine o'clock in the morning. When I arrived, he was standing with an elderly man who extended his hand.

"Hello, Mike," he said, "my name is Dick Salant."

I knew the name. For nearly twenty years, Richard Salant was the president of CBS News. He had recently left CBS to become a vice president with NBC News and was vacationing in Phoenix. Flipping through the channels of the hotel TV, he stopped when he saw the guy who didn't look or sound like anybody else.

"How would you like to work for NBC, Mike?"

"Well," I stammered. "I work for Mr. Chauncey. I have more than a year left on an agreement with the station, and . . ."

"Listen to the man," said Mr. Chauncey. "We don't want to lose you, but this kind of stuff never happens."

"But the two years . . . the money . . ."

My words weren't flowing. Mr. Chauncey put his hand up.

"Forget the money, son. You deserve this."

And that's how I came about getting my job with NBC News, less than two years after my friend Matt made the silly suggestion that someone like me could actually make it in television.

Twenty-five years later, my bosses at NBC News listened when I asked for time off to take my parents on one last trip around the country. Now I was steering the huge RV into a parking lot not far from my Winnetka, Illinois, home. Cathy, Megan, and Jamie were standing there with big smiles on their faces. We had made it back before the baby arrived. Now all we could do was wait.

And pray.

On the fourth day of March, my oldest daughter, Megan, checked into Chicago's Northwestern Memorial Hospital. This was her due date, and since the final ultrasound had detected little or no fetal weight gain in the last month of her pregnancy, Megan's doctor didn't want to take any more chances. Labor was induced at 8:00 A.M. Estimated time of birth: mid-afternoon.

At three o'clock, Jamie called to say that Meg was still in labor.

Four o'clock came and went.

Then five o'clock.

Jamie called again. The labor was dragging on.

Six o'clock.

Silence.

The phone rang. It was Mom calling from Kevin's house. What have you heard, she wanted to know.

"Nothing," I said.

"Jesus," she sighed.

At 7:00 P.M. Cathy, Kerry, Brendan, and I got in the car and headed toward Chicago, thirty minutes away. It was raining, and we inched along. During the quiet ride, a memory emerged. I saw Megan, eight years old, with the saddest look on her face. For weeks she had been begging for the gift of an umbrella, a clear plastic Hello Kitty umbrella. We finally got it for her, and Megan started praying for rain. The skies finally opened up and she ran outside, Hello Kitty umbrella in hand. I followed less than a minute later, anxious to see the joyous look on her face. By the time I got out to the front lawn she had already slipped and fallen on the slick grass. Her little hand gripped the bent and broken umbrella, now turned upside down. There were no tears, just a crest-fallen look that stayed burned into my brain. And that was just an umbrella.

An hour later, we parked our car near the hospital, and walked to a restaurant to eat and wait. Still no news. At nine-thirty we took our positions in the waiting room. What could be happening? Why hadn't we heard? Another hour of torture passed before Jamie finally appeared. He looked beat up . . . until he smiled.

"It's a girl," he said quietly. "And she's fine, just a little underweight."

Cathy and Kerry screamed with joy. Then Jamie spoke again.

"Six pounds, twelve ounces . . . twenty-and-a-half inches. And her name is Josephine."

He led us to the room and went in to see if Megan was ready for visitors. I entered first, struggling to focus my video camera through tear-filled eyes. Meg was smiling as I bent over to kiss her on the forehead and get a closer look at the perfect baby, wrapped in a blanket and cradled in her arms. Cathy and Kerry came through the door a few seconds later, walking side by side, holding their hands to their mouths in a futile attempt to control the sobbing. One by one the others took turns filing in—Brendan, Matt, and Margarita, a speechless procession of overwhelming happiness and relief.

The door squeaked open once more, followed by the sound of shuffling footsteps. A head peeked into the curtained-off area. It was my mother, her eyes searching the room for proof that the happy ending really existed. When the baby came into view, she raised a hand to her face and started to cry. The damaged heart had come to life after sixty years of painful silence. Moving from behind her, my father shook his head and quietly smiled, all of his prayers seemingly answered.

"We named her Josephine, after Jamie's grandmother," Megan explained. "We'll call her Josie."

"What's her middle name?" my mother asked.

"Her middle name," said Megan, "is Ann."

Dad put his arm around Mom—two old people holding each other for support while they stared through watery eyes at a sleeping baby, their first great-grandchild. One month in the life of one family. That's all it was. We had traveled nearly eight thousand miles, passing through eighteen states, searching for nothing in particular but finding something priceless.

A day after Josie's birth we gathered at Frank and Betsie's, a good restaurant in a neighboring village and the perfect setting to toast the end of the journey and the beginning of a new life. The restaurant is small and intimate. Sitting at a table by the front window, I could see cars driving by on the main street through town. None of those people, I mused, was the least bit affected by what we had just experienced. In the global picture, an average family celebrating the arrival of a baby is a trivial event. But when you add those trivial events up and then follow the lines connecting one small life to the next, the end result is often beyond your wildest imagination. Kerry worded it best when the dinner-table talk returned to the subject of newborn Josie.

"It's just amazing," she said with tears in her eyes, "that something so little is so big."

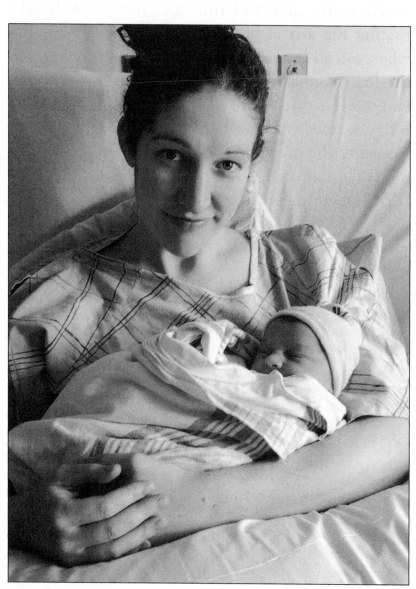

Megan and Josie.

Margarita, Marge, Matt, and Jack get their first close-up view.

The great-grandparents celebrate.

Mike and Josie.

The proud father—Jamie and Josie one year later.

Acknowledgments

This book wasn't my idea. The blame belongs to Jane Dystel, a New York City–based literary agent who called to ask if I was interested in turning my **Today** show musings into a book. I wasn't. That was twenty years ago. Most agents would have moved on but Jane hung in there, sending me a greeting card every Christmas. In December 2004 my card to her mentioned an upcoming RV journey with my parents, prompting a second call from Jane.

"That's your book," she said.

I took her word for it.

Now I'm an author, something nobody would have thought possible earlier in life. My flaws are many, my weaknesses painfully obvious. Jane saw merit where others didn't and for that I will never forget her. This book is full of people who came along just in time to help, inspire, even save me from a life of failure. Here are some who weren't mentioned.

Linda Marrow, my smart and funny editor at Ballantine had the confidence to let a "first timer" wing it. Her encouragement, suggestions, and laughter—and what a good laugh she has—kept me going.

NBC's Betsy Alexander, always in my corner, backed me once again when I called to say that my parents needed a chauffeur. She allowed me the time off and then OK'd my vague pitch about turning home movies from the journey into a four part **Today** show series. That kind of trust is rare in the TV business. Katie, Matt, Ann, Al, and Lester were kind in their praise of my parents, a wonderful gift that I can never repay.

Other NBC notables range from Steve Friedman who gave me the freedom to be different, to Jeff Zucker who pushed me to improve, to all the other producers who honored my desire to wander from the pack. Amy Wasserstrom, an NBC colleague and friend, became a sounding board for many of the stories that made it into this book, stories I would have forgotten to include without her prompting.

Stu Witt, my TV agent, deserves a mention just for being so entertaining over the last twenty years. He is one of the funniest people on earth and a good soul. Then there are my friends, hockey teammates, neighbors, and gym pals who helped guide me through this crazy project by lending an ear or reading excerpts. Their feedback was invaluable.

My family, of course, deserves the final bit of thanks. They are a nutty bunch but also a fountain of inspiration, all of them better than me in every meaningful way. To my parents, my brothers, my children, my daughter-in-law, my son-in-law, my granddaughter, and especially my wife, I bow in gratitude for your love and support.

ABOUT THE AUTHOR

MIKE LEONARD, a feature correspondent for NBC News, appears regularly on **Today**. He lives in Winnetka, Illinois. Mike Leonard and his wife Cathy are the parents of two daughters and two sons.